The Worship of Money

The Girl with the Yellow Clarinet or A
Course in Numerical Optimization

Hate for the stranger.If I was logical I would commit suicide.The only way to continue to live is madness.Expulsions of the Jews.Racial discrimination.It is close to the core of the human nature.The taboo of sexual choice.The depressive as a scapegoat.They accuse him of every mistake that happens.The foreign poor worker.The creation of illusions by the journalists.Can the cockroaches fly?The freaks don't have the intelligence to feel rejected,if they had it they would be depressed.What is postmodern realism?

Figureheads,thrown away like broken sculptures.The first meaning connects with the second meaning and they both create the paradox of algebraic forms.The topology of logical integrals is a numerical optimization.

Mamon,Amon,both shall arise to worship me.The freedom of human depends on his denial of God.The economics of the Underworld.Did Pluto deny his existence by saying lies to his closed ones?Forever younf or forever safe,at least until you die from unsafety.The pills work faster and faster never remembering but not forgeting the inevitable truth that to win the game is inevitable.He was so sure of his success ,he didn't have to pray to any God,he only optimized his life experience by maximizing hedonism.The optimization of pleasure means to increase knowledge.

The comparative study of the constitutions of the two major superpowers will unveil the secrets of their future strategy and behaviour.The analysis of the thinking patterns behind the creation of the two constitutions can lead us to create the new basic values of all the nations on earth and the constituion of the future space federation.We can why the two major superpowers have their power .Because of the design of their internal government.

What is material realism?The acceptance of the difference of values between the thief and the victim.Hate is the end of illusions.The ramifications of the apparent principles of society willlive forever inside the minds of the scholars.If you ask who is at the top of the pyramid,I will tell you it is Mamon the divine being who represents money and gold.He is the highest principlein this earth.Realism means to discover ways to win money for ourselves.What is hate if not the end of eternal truths and their substitution with aethereal entities of money and the pleasure of consumption.

An extreme point of a function is a point x which either maximizes or minimizes the value of a function.

This topic is broken into two major sub-problems:

1. Finding an extreme point of a real-valued function of a single variable, and
2. Finding an extreme point of a real-valued function of a many variables.

We will focus on finding local minima. If you want to adjust any of these methods for finding local maxima, recall that a local maxima of $f(x)$ is a local minima of $-f(x)$.

There are three techniques which we will cover which may be used to find the local minima of a univariate (single variable) function:

1. Golden-mean search
2. Newton's method
3. Quadratic optimization

Finding the local minima of a function of more than one variable may be done by using gradient descent. This technique converts the multi-variable problem into a univariate problem which we may solve using one of the above three techiques.

Each of these processes listed above are deterministic: given the same problem and the same initial conditions, they will always compute the same steps and converge to the same optimum. While such predictability is desirable in many engineering applications, it also carries a downside: given a problem with multiple local optima and only one global optimum, the methods will always converge to the optimum nearest to its initial conditions regardless of whether it is a local or global optimum.

In many engineering applications, the best system performance can only be achieved by discovering the global optimum. This requires methods that can diverge away from nearby local optima and explore the function space to converge on the global optimum. A deterministic method cannot do that: a method designed to converge will always converge on the first optimum it encounters, and a method designed to diverge from local optima will diverge from all optima.

The alternative to a deterministic method is a stochastic method: an algorithm that includes an element of randomness. This random element is what will allow the method to have two different behaviours, by giving it a chance to escape local optima but not the global optimum. This can be implemented in practice in a number of ways, such as for example by including a random variable in an equation or by having a decision step that includes an element of chance. It should be noted that a random element is not necessarily one whose value is a result of complete and unbiased chance, such as a lottery drawing. Rather, it is simply a term whose result is not known for sure in advance. It is completely acceptable to skew the probabilities towards a preferred outcome, or to change the probabilities as the algorithm progresses to reduce the impact of randomness over time. A flip of a coin with a 99-1 probability of landing on heads is still a stochastic event: even though one outcome is more likely than the other, it is still a result of chance.

Using randomness in our optimization algorithms eliminates some of the certainty we had with deterministic algorithms. As we've established, a stochastic algorithm is no longer guaranteed to converge on the nearest local optimum, which can be a desirable feature. However, this should not be mistaken for a certainty to converge on the global optimum; stochastic algorithms can make no such guarantee. Stochastic algorithms have a chance of avoiding a nearby local optimum and converging on the global optimum, which is more than can be said for a deterministic algorithm under the same conditions, with chance no outcome is certain. Another important difference is that running the same deterministic algorithm twice using the same data will lead to the exact same result, whereas doing this with a stochastic algorithm can lead to two very different results. The reason for this is of course the inclusion of a random element in the algorithm, which can take very different values in its various runs.

Stochastic optimization algorithms are an intense area of on-going research. Dozens of algorithms already exist, and new algorithms, variations, and enhancements are being proposed every year. Popular algorithms include genetic algorithms, ant colony algorithms, particle swarm algorithms, and many others. A complete review of these methods is beyond the scope of this book. We will limit ourselves to two stochastic optimization methods, to give an overview of this class of optimization methods.

Observation

We are looking for local extreme points. It is a very difficult to find global extreme points

A brute-force approach is any algorithm that tries possible solutions one after the other until it finds one that is acceptable or until a pre-set maximum number of attempts. A brute-force optimization algorithm would thus simply evaluate value after value for a given time, and return the value with the optimal result as its solution at the end. And a random brute-force search is one that selects the values to evaluate randomly.

While such a brute-force approach may seem unsophisticated, it does have the advantage of being able to search any function, even one that has a complex and irregular shape, multiple local optima, and even discontinuities. By trying points at random and always keeping the optimal one, it is likely to get close to the global optimum and certain not to get stuck in a local optimum. However, when it does get a point close to the global optimum, it does not improve on it except by possibly randomly generating an even closer point. In other words, while the random brute-force approach is likely to find a point close to the global optimum, it is very unlikely to actually find the global optimum itself. For that reason, the algorithm is often followed by a few iterations of a deterministic algorithm such as Newton's method, which can easily and quickly converge to the global optimum from the starting point found by the brute-force search.

It should be instinctively clear that testing more points increases the algorithm's odds of getting closer to the optimum. However, even that rule of thumb isn't guaranteed given the stochastic nature of the algorithm. It could easily be the case that in one short run the algorithm fortuitously generates a point very close to the optimum while in another much longer run the algorithm is a lot unluckier and doesn't get as close. This fact illustrates the unpredictability of working with stochastic algorithms.

Annealing

Annealing is a metallurgical process used to temper metals through a heating and cooling treatment. The weaknesses in the metal that are eliminated by annealing are the result of atomic irregularities in the crystalline structure of the metal. These irregularities are due to atoms being stuck in the wrong place of the structure. In the process of annealing, the metal is heated up and then allowed to cool down slowly. Heating up gives the atoms the energy they need to get un-stuck, and the slow cool-down period allows them to move to their correct location in the structure.

Annealing can be seen as a multiple-optima optimization problem. A weakness in the metal is due to an atom having converged on a local optimum in the metal's crystalline structure. Heating the metal gives that atom the ability to escape the local optimum, and the slow cool-down period allows it to converge on its global optimum.

Simulated Annealing

Simulated annealing is a stochastic optimization algorithm based on the observation we have made about the annealing process. Like the open deterministic optimization algorithms we have studied, it will iteratively improve a value by moving it step by step through the function space. However, in order to escape local optima, the algorithm will have a probability of taking a step in a bad direction: in other words, of taking a step that increases the value for a minimization problem or that decreases the value for a maximization problem. To simulate the annealing process, this probability will depend in part on a "temperature" parameter in the algorithm, which is initialized at a high value and decreased at each iteration. Consequently, the algorithm will initially have a high probability of moving away from a nearby (likely local) optimum. Over the iterations that probability will decrease and the algorithm will converge on the (hopefully global) optimum it did not have the chance to escape from.

The key to a successful simulated annealing algorithm is thus properly handling the "temperature" parameter. It should be high enough to allow the algorithm to escape local optima and decrease slowly enough to allow the algorithm to explore the search interval without getting stuck. However, it should not be set too high or remain at a high value for too long, to keep the algorithm from escaping the global optimum.

As we mentioned, the probability of accepting a step away from an optimum depends in part on the current value of the "temperature" parameter. The other factor it depends on is how much worse the new value would be after this step. The probability P of accepting a step away from an optimum is computed as:

$$P = e^{-\frac{\Delta f}{T}}$$

where T is the current temperature value and Δf is the difference between the previous and new value (or how much worse the value will be). By opposition, a step towards an optimum (which improves the value) should always be accepted.

The Constitution of the United States

Preamble

We the People of the United States, in Order to form a more perfect Union, establish Justice, insure domestic Tranquility, provide for the common defence, promote the general Welfare, and secure the Blessings of Liberty to ourselves and our Posterity, do ordain and establish this Constitution for the United States of America.

Article I - The Legislative Branch

Section 1 - The Legislature

All legislative Powers herein granted shall be vested in a Congress of the United States, which shall consist of a Senate and House of Representatives.

Section 2 - The House

The House of Representatives shall be composed of Members chosen every second Year by the People of the several States, and the Electors in each State shall have the Qualifications requisite for Electors of the most numerous Branch of the State Legislature.

No Person shall be a Representative who shall not have attained to the Age of twenty five Years, and been seven Years a Citizen of the United States, and who shall not, when elected, be an Inhabitant of that State in which he shall be chosen.

(Representatives and direct Taxes shall be apportioned among the several States which may be included within this Union, according to their respective Numbers, which shall be determined by adding to the whole Number of free Persons, including those bound to Service for a Term of Years, and excluding Indians not taxed, three fifths of all other Persons.) The actual Enumeration shall be made within three Years after the first Meeting of the Congress of the United States, and within every subsequent Term of ten Years, in such Manner as they shall by Law direct. The Number of Representatives shall not exceed one for every thirty Thousand, but each State shall have at Least one Representative; and until such enumeration shall be made, the State of New Hampshire shall be entitled to chuse three, Massachusetts eight, Rhode Island and Providence Plantations one, Connecticut five, New York six, New Jersey four, Pennsylvania eight, Delaware one, Maryland six, Virginia ten, North Carolina five, South Carolina five and Georgia three.

When vacancies happen in the Representation from any State, the Executive Authority thereof shall issue Writs of Election to fill such Vacancies.

The House of Representatives shall chuse their Speaker and other Officers; and shall have the sole Power of Impeachment.

Section 3 - The Senate

The Senate of the United States shall be composed of two Senators from each State, for six Years; and each Senator shall have one Vote.

Immediately after they shall be assembled in Consequence of the first Election, they shall be divided as equally as may be into three Classes. The Seats of the Senators of the first Class shall be vacated at the Expiration of the second Year, of the second Class at the Expiration of the fourth Year, and of the third Class at the Expiration of the sixth Year, so that one third may be chosen every second Year; *(and if Vacancies happen by Resignation, or otherwise, during the Recess of the Legislature of any State, the Executive thereof may make temporary Appointments until the next Meeting of the Legislature, which shall then fill such Vacancies.)*No person shall be a Senator who shall not have attained to the Age of thirty Years, and been nine Years a Citizen of the United States, and who shall not, when elected, be an Inhabitant of that State for which he shall be chosen.

The Vice President of the United States shall be President of the Senate, but shall have no Vote, unless they be equally divided.

The Senate shall chuse their other Officers, and also a President pro tempore, in the absence of the Vice President, or when he shall exercise the Office of President of the United States.

The Senate shall have the sole Power to try all Impeachments. When sitting for that Purpose, they shall be on Oath or Affirmation. When the President of the United States is tried, the Chief Justice shall preside: And no Person shall be convicted without the Concurrence of two thirds of the Members present.

Judgment in Cases of Impeachment shall not extend further than to removal from Office, and disqualification to hold and enjoy any Office of honor, Trust or Profit under the United States: but the Party convicted shall nevertheless be liable and subject to Indictment, Trial, Judgment and Punishment, according to Law.

Section 4 - Elections, Meetings

The Times, Places and Manner of holding Elections for Senators and Representatives, shall be prescribed in each State by the Legislature thereof; but the Congress may at any time by Law make or alter such Regulations, except as to the Place of Chusing Senators.

The Congress shall assemble at least once in every Year, and such Meeting shall *(be on the first Monday in December,)*) unless they shall by Law appoint a different Day.

Section 5 - Membership, Rules, Journals,

Each House shall be the Judge of the Elections, Returns and Qualifications of its own Members, and a Majority of each shall constitute a Quorum to do Business; but a smaller number may adjourn from day to day, and may be authorized to compel the Attendance of absent Members, in such Manner, and under such Penalties as each House may provide.

Each House may determine the Rules of its Proceedings, punish its Members for disorderly Behavior, and, with the Concurrence of two-thirds, expel a Member.

Each House shall keep a Journal of its Proceedings, and from time to time publish the same, excepting such Parts as may in their Judgment require Secrecy; and the Yeas and Nays of the Members of either House on any question shall, at the Desire of one fifth of those Present, be entered on the Journal.

Neither House, during the Session of Congress, shall, without the Consent of the other, adjourn for more than three days, nor to any other Place than that in which the two Houses shall be sitting.

Section 6 - Compensation

(The Senators and Representatives shall receive a Compensation for their Services, to be ascertained by Law, and paid out of the Treasury of the United States.) They shall in all Cases, except Treason, Felony and Breach of the Peace, be privileged from Arrest during their Attendance at the Session of their respective Houses, and in going to and returning from the same; and for any Speech or Debate in either House, they shall not be questioned in any other Place.

No Senator or Representative shall, during the Time for which he was elected, be appointed to any civil Office under the Authority of the United States which shall have been created, or the Emoluments whereof shall have been increased during such time; and no

Person holding any Office under the United States, shall be a Member of either House during his Continuance in Office.

Section 7 - Revenue Bills, Legislative Process, Presidential Veto

All bills for raising Revenue shall originate in the House of Representatives; but the Senate may propose or concur with Amendments as on other Bills.

Every Bill which shall have passed the House of Representatives and the Senate, shall, before it become a Law, be presented to the President of the United States; If he approve he shall sign it, but if not he shall return it, with his Objections to that House in which it shall have originated, who shall enter the Objections at large on their Journal, and proceed to reconsider it. If after such Reconsideration two thirds of that House shall agree to pass the Bill, it shall be sent, together with the Objections, to the other House, by which it shall likewise be reconsidered, and if approved by two thirds of that House, it shall become a Law. But in all such Cases the Votes of both Houses shall be determined by Yeas and Nays, and the Names of the Persons voting for and against the Bill shall be entered on the Journal of each House respectively. If any Bill shall not be returned by the President within ten Days (Sundays excepted) after it shall have been presented to him, the Same shall be a Law, in like Manner as if he had signed it, unless the Congress by their Adjournment prevent its Return, in which Case it shall not be a Law.

Every Order, Resolution, or Vote to which the
Concurrence of the Senate and House of
Representatives may be necessary (except on a
question of Adjournment) shall be presented to the
President of the United States; and before the Same
shall take Effect, shall be approved by him, or being
disapproved by him, shall be repassed by two thirds
of the Senate and House of Representatives,
according to the Rules and Limitations prescribed in
the Case of a Bill.

Section 8 - Powers of Congress

The Congress shall have Power To lay and collect
Taxes, Duties, Imposts and Excises, to pay the Debts
and provide for the common Defence and general
Welfare of the United States; but all Duties, Imposts
and Excises shall be uniform throughout the United
States;

To borrow money on the credit of the United States;

To regulate Commerce with foreign Nations, and
among the several States, and with the Indian Tribes;

To establish an uniform Rule of Naturalization, and
uniform Laws on the subject of Bankruptcies
throughout the United States;

To coin Money, regulate the Value thereof, and of
foreign Coin, and fix the Standard of Weights and
Measures;

To provide for the Punishment of counterfeiting the Securities and current Coin of the United States;

To establish Post Offices and Post Roads;

To promote the Progress of Science and useful Arts, by securing for limited Times to Authors and Inventors the exclusive Right to their respective Writings and Discoveries;

To constitute Tribunals inferior to the supreme Court;

To define and punish Piracies and Felonies committed on the high Seas, and Offenses against the Law of Nations;

To declare War, grant Letters of Marque and Reprisal, and make Rules concerning Captures on Land and Water;

To raise and support Armies, but no Appropriation of Money to that Use shall be for a longer Term than two Years;

To provide and maintain a Navy;

To make Rules for the Government and Regulation of the land and naval Forces;

To provide for calling forth the Militia to execute the Laws of the Union, suppress Insurrections and repel Invasions;

To provide for organizing, arming, and disciplining, the Militia, and for governing such Part of them as may be employed in the Service of the United States, reserving to the States respectively, the Appointment of the Officers, and the Authority of training the Militia according to the discipline prescribed by Congress;

To exercise exclusive Legislation in all Cases whatsoever, over such District (not exceeding ten Miles square) as may, by Cession of particular States, and the acceptance of Congress, become the Seat of the Government of the United States, and to exercise like Authority over all Places purchased by the Consent of the Legislature of the State in which the Same shall be, for the Erection of Forts, Magazines, Arsenals, dock-Yards, and other needful Buildings; And

To make all Laws which shall be necessary and proper for carrying into Execution the foregoing Powers, and all other Powers vested by this Constitution in the Government of the United States, or in any Department or Officer thereof.

Section 9 - Limits on Congress

The Migration or Importation of such Persons as any of the States now existing shall think proper to admit, shall not be prohibited by the Congress prior to the Year one thousand eight hundred and eight, but a tax or duty may be imposed on such Importation, not exceeding ten dollars for each Person.

The privilege of the Writ of Habeas Corpus shall not be suspended, unless when in Cases of Rebellion or Invasion the public Safety may require it.

No Bill of Attainder or ex post facto Law shall be passed.

(No capitation, or other direct, Tax shall be laid, unless in Proportion to the Census or Enumeration herein before directed to be taken.)

No Tax or Duty shall be laid on Articles exported from any State.

No Preference shall be given by any Regulation of Commerce or Revenue to the Ports of one State over those of another: nor shall Vessels bound to, or from, one State, be obliged to enter, clear, or pay Duties in another.

No Money shall be drawn from the Treasury, but in Consequence of Appropriations made by Law; and a regular Statement and Account of the Receipts and Expenditures of all public Money shall be published from time to time.

No Title of Nobility shall be granted by the United States: And no Person holding any Office of Profit or Trust under them, shall, without the Consent of the Congress, accept of any present, Emolument, Office, or Title, of any kind whatever, from any King, Prince or foreign State.

Section 10 - Powers prohibited of States

No State shall enter into any Treaty, Alliance, or Confederation; grant Letters of Marque and Reprisal; coin Money; emit Bills of Credit; make any Thing but gold and silver Coin a Tender in Payment of Debts; pass any Bill of Attainder, ex post facto Law, or Law impairing the Obligation of Contracts, or grant any Title of Nobility.

No State shall, without the Consent of the Congress, lay any Imposts or Duties on Imports or Exports, except what may be absolutely necessary for executing it's inspection Laws: and the net Produce of all Duties and Imposts, laid by any State on Imports or Exports, shall be for the Use of the Treasury of the United States; and all such Laws shall be subject to the Revision and Controul of the Congress.

No State shall, without the Consent of Congress, lay any duty of Tonnage, keep Troops, or Ships of War in time of Peace, enter into any Agreement or Compact with another State, or with a foreign Power, or engage in War, unless actually invaded, or in such imminent Danger as will not admit of delay.

Article II - The Executive Branch

Section 1 - The President

The executive Power shall be vested in a President of the United States of America. He shall hold his Office during the Term of four Years, and, together with the Vice-President chosen for the same Term, be elected, as follows:

Each State shall appoint, in such Manner as the Legislature thereof may direct, a Number of Electors, equal to the whole Number of Senators and Representatives to which the State may be entitled in the Congress: but no Senator or Representative, or Person holding an Office of Trust or Profit under the United States, shall be appointed an Elector.

(The Electors shall meet in their respective States, and vote by Ballot for two persons, of whom one at least shall not lie an Inhabitant of the same State with themselves. And they shall make a List of all the Persons voted for, and of the Number of Votes for each; which List they shall sign and certify, and transmit sealed to the Seat of the Government of the United States, directed to the President of the Senate. The President of the Senate shall, in the Presence of the Senate and House of Representatives, open all the Certificates, and the Votes shall then be counted. The Person having the greatest Number of Votes shall be the President, if such Number be a Majority of the whole Number of Electors appointed; and if there be more than one who have such Majority, and have an equal Number of Votes, then the House of Representatives shall immediately chuse by Ballot one of them for President; and if no Person have a Majority, then from the five highest on the List the said House shall in like Manner chuse the President. But in chusing the President, the Votes shall be taken by States, the Representation from each State having one Vote; a quorum for this Purpose shall consist of a Member or Members from two-thirds of the States, and a Majority of all the States shall be necessary to a Choice. In every Case, after the Choice of the President, the Person having the greatest Number of

Votes of the Electors shall be the Vice President. But if there should remain two or more who have equal Votes, the Senate shall chuse from them by Ballot the Vice-President.)

The Congress may determine the Time of chusing the Electors, and the Day on which they shall give their Votes; which Day shall be the same throughout the United States.

No person except a natural born Citizen, or a Citizen of the United States, at the time of the Adoption of this Constitution, shall be eligible to the Office of President; neither shall any Person be eligible to that Office who shall not have attained to the Age of thirty-five Years, and been fourteen Years a Resident within the United States.

(In Case of the Removal of the President from Office, or of his Death, Resignation, or Inability to discharge the Powers and Duties of the said Office, the same shall devolve on the Vice President, and the Congress may by Law provide for the Case of Removal, Death, Resignation or Inability, both of the President and Vice President, declaring what Officer shall then act as President, and such Officer shall act accordingly, until the Disability be removed, or a President shall be elected.)

The President shall, at stated Times, receive for his Services, a Compensation, which shall neither be increased nor diminished during the Period for which he shall have been elected, and he shall not receive within that Period any other Emolument from the United States, or any of them.

Before he enter on the Execution of his Office, he shall take the following Oath or Affirmation:

"I do solemnly swear (or affirm) that I will faithfully execute the Office of President of the United States, and will to the best of my Ability, preserve, protect and defend the Constitution of the United States."

Section 2 - Civilian Power over Military, Cabinet, Pardon Power, Appointments

The President shall be Commander in Chief of the Army and Navy of the United States, and of the Militia of the several States, when called into the actual Service of the United States; he may require the Opinion, in writing, of the principal Officer in each of the executive Departments, upon any subject relating to the Duties of their respective Offices, and he shall have Power to Grant Reprieves and Pardons for Offenses against the United States, except in Cases of Impeachment.

He shall have Power, by and with the Advice and Consent of the Senate, to make Treaties, provided two thirds of the Senators present concur; and he shall nominate, and by and with the Advice and Consent of the Senate, shall appoint Ambassadors, other public Ministers and Consuls, Judges of the supreme Court, and all other Officers of the United States, whose Appointments are not herein otherwise provided for, and which shall be established by Law: but the Congress may by Law vest the Appointment of such inferior Officers, as they think proper, in the President alone, in the Courts of Law, or in the Heads of Departments.

The President shall have Power to fill up all Vacancies that may happen during the Recess of the Senate, by granting Commissions which shall expire at the End of their next Session.

Section 3 - State of the Union, Convening Congress

He shall from time to time give to the Congress Information of the State of the Union, and recommend to their Consideration such Measures as he shall judge necessary and expedient; he may, on extraordinary Occasions, convene both Houses, or either of them, and in Case of Disagreement between them, with Respect to the Time of Adjournment, he may adjourn them to such Time as he shall think proper; he shall receive Ambassadors and other public Ministers; he shall take Care that the Laws be faithfully executed, and shall Commission all the Officers of the United States.

Section 4 - Disqualification

The President, Vice President and all civil Officers of the United States, shall be removed from Office on Impeachment for, and Conviction of, Treason, Bribery, or other high Crimes and Misdemeanors.

Article III - The Judicial Branch

Section 1 - Judicial powers

The judicial Power of the United States, shall be vested in one supreme Court, and in such inferior Courts as the Congress may from time to time ordain and establish. The Judges, both of the supreme and inferior Courts, shall hold their Offices during good Behavior, and shall, at stated Times, receive for their Services a Compensation which shall not be diminished during their Continuance in Office.

Section 2 - Trial by Jury, Original Jurisdiction, Jury Trials

(The judicial Power shall extend to all Cases, in Law and Equity, arising under this Constitution, the Laws of the United States, and Treaties made, or which shall be made, under their Authority; to all Cases affecting Ambassadors, other public Ministers and Consuls; to all Cases of admiralty and maritime Jurisdiction; to Controversies to which the United States shall be a Party; to Controversies between two or more States; between a State and Citizens of another State; between Citizens of different States; between Citizens of the same State claiming Lands under Grants of different States, and between a State, or the Citizens thereof, and foreign States, Citizens or Subjects.)

In all Cases affecting Ambassadors, other public Ministers and Consuls, and those in which a State shall be Party, the supreme Court shall have original Jurisdiction. In all the other Cases before mentioned, the supreme Court shall have appellate Jurisdiction, both as to Law and Fact, with such Exceptions, and under such Regulations as the Congress shall make.

The Trial of all Crimes, except in Cases of Impeachment, shall be by Jury; and such Trial shall be held in the State where the said Crimes shall have been committed; but when not committed within any State, the Trial shall be at such Place or Places as the Congress may by Law have directed.

Section 3 - Treason *Note*

Treason against the United States, shall consist only in levying War against them, or in adhering to their Enemies, giving them Aid and Comfort. No Person shall be convicted of Treason unless on the Testimony of two Witnesses to the same overt Act, or on Confession in open Court.

The Congress shall have power to declare the Punishment of Treason, but no Attainder of Treason shall work Corruption of Blood, or Forfeiture except during the Life of the Person attainted.

Article IV - The States

Section 1 - Each State to Honor all others

Full Faith and Credit shall be given in each State to the public Acts, Records, and judicial Proceedings of every other State. And the Congress may by general Laws prescribe the Manner in which such Acts, Records and Proceedings shall be proved, and the Effect thereof.

Section 2 - State citizens, Extradition

The Citizens of each State shall be entitled to all Privileges and Immunities of Citizens in the several States.

A Person charged in any State with Treason, Felony, or other Crime, who shall flee from Justice, and be found in another State, shall on demand of the executive Authority of the State from which he fled, be delivered up, to be removed to the State having Jurisdiction of the Crime.

(No Person held to Service or Labour in one State, under the Laws thereof, escaping into another, shall, in Consequence of any Law or Regulation therein, be discharged from such Service or Labour, But shall be delivered up on Claim of the Party to whom such Service or Labour may be due

Section 3 - New States

New States may be admitted by the Congress into this Union; but no new States shall be formed or erected within the Jurisdiction of any other State; nor any State be formed by the Junction of two or more States, or parts of States, without the Consent of the Legislatures of the States concerned as well as of the Congress.

The Congress shall have Power to dispose of and make all needful Rules and Regulations respecting the Territory or other Property belonging to the United States; and nothing in this Constitution shall be so construed as to Prejudice any Claims of the United States, or of any particular State.

Section 4 - Republican government

The United States shall guarantee to every State in this Union a Republican Form of Government, and shall protect each of them against Invasion; and on Application of the Legislature, or of the Executive (when the Legislature cannot be convened) against domestic Violence.

Article V - Amendment

The Congress, whenever two thirds of both Houses shall deem it necessary, shall propose Amendments to this Constitution, or, on the Application of the Legislatures of two thirds of the several States, shall call a Convention for proposing Amendments, which, in either Case, shall be valid to all Intents and Purposes, as part of this Constitution, when ratified by the Legislatures of three fourths of the several States, or by Conventions in three fourths thereof, as the one or the other Mode of Ratification may be proposed by the Congress; Provided that no Amendment which may be made prior to the Year One thousand eight hundred and eight shall in any Manner affect the first and fourth Clauses in the Ninth Section of the first Article; and that no State, without its Consent, shall be deprived of its equal Suffrage in the Senate.

Article VI - Debts, Supremacy, Oaths

All Debts contracted and Engagements entered into, before the Adoption of this Constitution, shall be as valid against the United States under this Constitution, as under the Confederation.

This Constitution, and the Laws of the United States which shall be made in Pursuance thereof; and all Treaties made, or which shall be made, under the Authority of the United States, shall be the supreme Law of the Land; and the Judges in every State shall be bound thereby, any Thing in the Constitution or Laws of any State to the Contrary notwithstanding.

The Senators and Representatives before mentioned, and the Members of the several State Legislatures, and all executive and judicial Officers, both of the United States and of the several States, shall be bound by Oath or Affirmation, to support this Constitution; but no religious Test shall ever be required as a Qualification to any Office or public Trust under the United States.

Article VII - Ratification *Documents*

The Ratification of the Conventions of nine States, shall be sufficient for the Establishment of this Constitution between the States so ratifying the Same.

Done in Convention by the Unanimous Consent of the States present the Seventeenth Day of September in the Year of our Lord one thousand seven hundred and Eighty seven and of the Independence of the United States of America the Twelfth. In Witness whereof We have hereunto subscribed our Names.

Go Washington - President and deputy from Virginia

New Hampshire - John Langdon, Nicholas Gilman

Massachusetts - Nathaniel Gorham, Rufus King

Connecticut - Wm Saml Johnson, Roger Sherman

New York - Alexander Hamilton

New Jersey - Wil Livingston, David Brearley, Wm Paterson, Jona. Dayton

Pensylvania - B Franklin, Thomas Mifflin, Robt Morris, Geo. Clymer, Thos FitzSimons, Jared Ingersoll, James Wilson, Gouv Morris

Delaware - Geo. Read, Gunning Bedford jun, John Dickinson, Richard Bassett, Jaco. Broom

Maryland - James McHenry, Dan of St Tho Jenifer, Danl Carroll

Virginia - John Blair, James Madison Jr.

North Carolina - Wm Blount, Richd Dobbs Spaight, Hu Williamson

South Carolina - J. Rutledge, Charles Cotesworth Pinckney, Charles Pinckney, Pierce Butler

Georgia - William Few, Abr Baldwin

Attest: William Jackson, Secretary

The Amendments

Amendment 1 - Freedom of Religion, Press, Expression. Ratified 12/15/1791.

Congress shall make no law respecting an establishment of religion, or prohibiting the free exercise thereof; or abridging the freedom of speech, or of the press; or the right of the people peaceably to assemble, and to petition the Government for a redress of grievances.

Amendment 2 - Right to Bear Arms. Ratified 12/15/1791.

A well regulated Militia, being necessary to the security of a free State, the right of the people to keep and bear Arms, shall not be infringed.

Amendment 3 - Quartering of Soldiers. Ratified
12/15/1791.

No Soldier shall, in time of peace be quartered in any
house, without the consent of the Owner, nor in time
of war, but in a manner to be prescribed by law.

Amendment 4 - Search and Seizure. Ratified
12/15/1791.

The right of the people to be secure in their persons,
houses, papers, and effects, against unreasonable
searches and seizures, shall not be violated, and no
Warrants shall issue, but upon probable cause,
supported by Oath or affirmation, and particularly
describing the place to be searched, and the persons or
things to be seized.

Amendment 5 - Trial and Punishment, Compensation
for Takings. Ratified 12/15/1791.

No person shall be held to answer for a capital, or
otherwise infamous crime, unless on a presentment or
indictment of a Grand Jury, except in cases arising in
the land or naval forces, or in the Militia, when in
actual service in time of War or public danger; nor
shall any person be subject for the same offense to be
twice put in jeopardy of life or limb; nor shall be
compelled in any criminal case to be a witness against
himself, nor be deprived of life, liberty, or property,

without due process of law; nor shall private property be taken for public use, without just compensation.

Amendment 6 - Right to Speedy Trial, Confrontation of Witnesses. Ratified 12/15/1791.

In all criminal prosecutions, the accused shall enjoy the right to a speedy and public trial, by an impartial jury of the State and district wherein the crime shall have been committed, which district shall have been previously ascertained by law, and to be informed of the nature and cause of the accusation; to be confronted with the witnesses against him; to have compulsory process for obtaining witnesses in his favor, and to have the Assistance of Counsel for his defence.

Amendment 7 - Trial by Jury in Civil Cases. Ratified 12/15/1791.

In Suits at common law, where the value in controversy shall exceed twenty dollars, the right of trial by jury shall be preserved, and no fact tried by a jury, shall be otherwise re-examined in any Court of the United States, than according to the rules of the common law.

Amendment 8 - Cruel and Unusual Punishment.
Ratified 12/15/1791.

Excessive bail shall not be required, nor excessive
fines imposed, nor cruel and unusual punishments
inflicted.

Amendment 9 - Construction of Constitution. Ratified
12/15/1791.

The enumeration in the Constitution, of certain rights,
shall not be construed to deny or disparage others
retained by the people.

Amendment 10 - Powers of the States and People.
Ratified 12/15/1791.

The powers not delegated to the United States by the
Constitution, nor prohibited by it to the States, are
reserved to the States respectively, or to the people.

Amendment 11 - Judicial Limits. Ratified 2/7/1795.

The Judicial power of the United States shall not be
construed to extend to any suit in law or equity,
commenced or prosecuted against one of the United
States by Citizens of another State, or by Citizens or
Subjects of any Foreign State.

Amendment 12 - Choosing the President, Vice-President. Ratified 6/15/1804.

The Electors shall meet in their respective states, and vote by ballot for President and Vice-President, one of whom, at least, shall not be an inhabitant of the same state with themselves; they shall name in their ballots the person voted for as President, and in distinct ballots the person voted for as Vice-President, and they shall make distinct lists of all persons voted for as President, and of all persons voted for as Vice-President and of the number of votes for each, which lists they shall sign and certify, and transmit sealed to the seat of the government of the United States, directed to the President of the Senate;

The President of the Senate shall, in the presence of the Senate and House of Representatives, open all the certificates and the votes shall then be counted;

The person having the greatest Number of votes for President, shall be the President, if such number be a majority of the whole number of Electors appointed; and if no person have such majority, then from the persons having the highest numbers not exceeding three on the list of those voted for as President, the House of Representatives shall choose immediately, by ballot, the President. But in choosing the President, the votes shall be taken by states, the representation from each state having one vote; a quorum for this purpose shall consist of a member or members from two-thirds of the states, and a majority of all the states shall be necessary to a choice. And if the House of

Representatives shall not choose a President whenever the right of choice shall devolve upon them, before the fourth day of March next following, then the Vice-President shall act as President, as in the case of the death or other constitutional disability of the President.

The person having the greatest number of votes as Vice-President, shall be the Vice-President, if such number be a majority of the whole number of Electors appointed, and if no person have a majority, then from the two highest numbers on the list, the Senate shall choose the Vice-President; a quorum for the purpose shall consist of two-thirds of the whole number of Senators, and a majority of the whole number shall be necessary to a choice. But no person constitutionally ineligible to the office of President shall be eligible to that of Vice-President of the United States.

Amendment 13 - Slavery Abolished. Ratified 12/6/1865.

1. Neither slavery nor involuntary servitude, except as a punishment for crime whereof the party shall have been duly convicted, shall exist within the United States, or any place subject to their jurisdiction.

2. Congress shall have power to enforce this article by appropriate legislation.

Amendment 14 - Citizenship Rights. Ratified 7/9/1868.

1. All persons born or naturalized in the United States, and subject to the jurisdiction thereof, are citizens of the United States and of the State wherein they reside. No State shall make or enforce any law which shall abridge the privileges or immunities of citizens of the United States; nor shall any State deprive any person of life, liberty, or property, without due process of law; nor deny to any person within its jurisdiction the equal protection of the laws.

2. Representatives shall be apportioned among the several States according to their respective numbers, counting the whole number of persons in each State, excluding Indians not taxed. But when the right to vote at any election for the choice of electors for President and Vice-President of the United States, Representatives in Congress, the Executive and Judicial officers of a State, or the members of the Legislature thereof, is denied to any of the male inhabitants of such State, being twenty-one years of age, and citizens of the United States, or in any way abridged, except for participation in rebellion, or other crime, the basis of representation therein shall be reduced in the proportion which the number of such male citizens shall bear to the whole number of male citizens twenty-one years of age in such State.

3. No person shall be a Senator or Representative in Congress, or elector of President and Vice-President, or hold any office, civil or military, under the United States, or under any State, who, having previously taken an oath, as a member of Congress, or as an

officer of the United States, or as a member of any State legislature, or as an executive or judicial officer of any State, to support the Constitution of the United States, shall have engaged in insurrection or rebellion against the same, or given aid or comfort to the enemies thereof. But Congress may by a vote of two-thirds of each House, remove such disability.

4. The validity of the public debt of the United States, authorized by law, including debts incurred for payment of pensions and bounties for services in suppressing insurrection or rebellion, shall not be questioned. But neither the United States nor any State shall assume or pay any debt or obligation incurred in aid of insurrection or rebellion against the United States, or any claim for the loss or emancipation of any slave; but all such debts, obligations and claims shall be held illegal and void.

5. The Congress shall have power to enforce, by appropriate legislation, the provisions of this article.

Amendment 15 - Race No Bar to Vote. Ratified 2/3/1870.

1. The right of citizens of the United States to vote shall not be denied or abridged by the United States or by any State on account of race, color, or previous condition of servitude.

2. The Congress shall have power to enforce this article by appropriate legislation.

Amendment 16 - Status of Income Tax Clarified. Ratified 2/3/1913.

The Congress shall have power to lay and collect taxes on incomes, from whatever source derived, without apportionment among the several States, and without regard to any census or enumeration.

Amendment 17 - Senators Elected by Popular Vote. Ratified 4/8/1913.

The Senate of the United States shall be composed of two Senators from each State, elected by the people thereof, for six years; and each Senator shall have one vote. The electors in each State shall have the qualifications requisite for electors of the most numerous branch of the State legislatures.

When vacancies happen in the representation of any State in the Senate, the executive authority of such State shall issue writs of election to fill such vacancies: Provided, That the legislature of any State may empower the executive thereof to make temporary appointments until the people fill the vacancies by election as the legislature may direct.

This amendment shall not be so construed as to affect the election or term of any Senator chosen before it becomes valid as part of the Constitution.

Amendment 18 - Liquor Abolished. Ratified 1/16/1919. Repealed by Amendment 21, 12/5/1933.

1. After one year from the ratification of this article the manufacture, sale, or transportation of intoxicating liquors within, the importation thereof into, or the exportation thereof from the United States and all territory subject to the jurisdiction thereof for beverage purposes is hereby prohibited.

2. The Congress and the several States shall have concurrent power to enforce this article by appropriate legislation.

3. This article shall be inoperative unless it shall have been ratified as an amendment to the Constitution by the legislatures of the several States, as provided in the Constitution, within seven years from the date of the submission hereof to the States by the Congress.

Amendment 19 - Women's Suffrage. Ratified 8/18/1920.

The right of citizens of the United States to vote shall not be denied or abridged by the United States or by any State on account of sex.

Congress shall have power to enforce this article by appropriate legislation.

Amendment 20 - Presidential, Congressional Terms.
Ratified 1/23/1933.

1. The terms of the President and Vice President shall
end at noon on the 20th day of January, and the terms
of Senators and Representatives at noon on the 3d day
of January, of the years in which such terms would
have ended if this article had not been ratified; and the
terms of their successors shall then begin.

2. The Congress shall assemble at least once in every
year, and such meeting shall begin at noon on the 3d
day of January, unless they shall by law appoint a
different day.

3. If, at the time fixed for the beginning of the term of
the President, the President elect shall have died, the
Vice President elect shall become President. If a
President shall not have been chosen before the time
fixed for the beginning of his term, or if the President
elect shall have failed to qualify, then the Vice
President elect shall act as President until a President
shall have qualified; and the Congress may by law
provide for the case wherein neither a President elect
nor a Vice President elect shall have qualified,
declaring who shall then act as President, or the
manner in which one who is to act shall be selected,
and such person shall act accordingly until a President
or Vice President shall have qualified.

4. The Congress may by law provide for the case of
the death of any of the persons from whom the House
of Representatives may choose a President whenever

the right of choice shall have devolved upon them, and for the case of the death of any of the persons from whom the Senate may choose a Vice President whenever the right of choice shall have devolved upon them.

5. Sections 1 and 2 shall take effect on the 15th day of October following the ratification of this article.

6. This article shall be inoperative unless it shall have been ratified as an amendment to the Constitution by the legislatures of three-fourths of the several States within seven years from the date of its submission.

Amendment 21 - Amendment 18 Repealed. Ratified 12/5/1933.

1. The eighteenth article of amendment to the Constitution of the United States is hereby repealed.

2. The transportation or importation into any State, Territory, or possession of the United States for delivery or use therein of intoxicating liquors, in violation of the laws thereof, is hereby prohibited.

3. The article shall be inoperative unless it shall have been ratified as an amendment to the Constitution by conventions in the several States, as provided in the Constitution, within seven years from the date of the submission hereof to the States by the Congress.

Amendment 22 - Presidential Term Limits. Ratified 2/27/1951.

1. No person shall be elected to the office of the President more than twice, and no person who has held the office of President, or acted as President, for more than two years of a term to which some other person was elected President shall be elected to the office of the President more than once. But this Article shall not apply to any person holding the office of President, when this Article was proposed by the Congress, and shall not prevent any person who may be holding the office of President, or acting as President, during the term within which this Article becomes operative from holding the office of President or acting as President during the remainder of such term.

2. This article shall be inoperative unless it shall have been ratified as an amendment to the Constitution by the legislatures of three-fourths of the several States within seven years from the date of its submission to the States by the Congress.

Amendment 23 - Presidential Vote for District of Columbia. Ratified 3/29/1961.

1. The District constituting the seat of Government of the United States shall appoint in such manner as the Congress may direct: A number of electors of President and Vice President equal to the whole number of Senators and Representatives in Congress to which the District would be entitled if it were a

State, but in no event more than the least populous State; they shall be in addition to those appointed by the States, but they shall be considered, for the purposes of the election of President and Vice President, to be electors appointed by a State; and they shall meet in the District and perform such duties as provided by the twelfth article of amendment.

2. The Congress shall have power to enforce this article by appropriate legislation.

Amendment 24 - Poll Tax Barred. Ratified 1/23/1964.

1. The right of citizens of the United States to vote in any primary or other election for President or Vice President, for electors for President or Vice President, or for Senator or Representative in Congress, shall not be denied or abridged by the United States or any State by reason of failure to pay any poll tax or other tax.

2. The Congress shall have power to enforce this article by appropriate legislation.

Amendment 25 - Presidential Disability and Succession. Ratified 2/10/1967.

1. In case of the removal of the President from office or of his death or resignation, the Vice President shall become President.

2. Whenever there is a vacancy in the office of the Vice President, the President shall nominate a Vice President who shall take office upon confirmation by a majority vote of both Houses of Congress.

3. Whenever the President transmits to the President pro tempore of the Senate and the Speaker of the House of Representatives his written declaration that he is unable to discharge the powers and duties of his office, and until he transmits to them a written declaration to the contrary, such powers and duties shall be discharged by the Vice President as Acting President.

4. Whenever the Vice President and a majority of either the principal officers of the executive departments or of such other body as Congress may by law provide, transmit to the President pro tempore of the Senate and the Speaker of the House of Representatives their written declaration that the President is unable to discharge the powers and duties of his office, the Vice President shall immediately assume the powers and duties of the office as Acting President.

Thereafter, when the President transmits to the President pro tempore of the Senate and the Speaker of the House of Representatives his written declaration that no inability exists, he shall resume the powers and duties of his office unless the Vice President and a majority of either the principal officers of the executive department or of such other body as Congress may by law provide, transmit within four days to the President pro tempore of the Senate and the Speaker of the House of

Representatives their written declaration that the President is unable to discharge the powers and duties of his office. Thereupon Congress shall decide the issue, assembling within forty eight hours for that purpose if not in session. If the Congress, within twenty one days after receipt of the latter written declaration, or, if Congress is not in session, within twenty one days after Congress is required to assemble, determines by two thirds vote of both Houses that the President is unable to discharge the powers and duties of his office, the Vice President shall continue to discharge the same as Acting President; otherwise, the President shall resume the powers and duties of his office.

Amendment 26 - Voting Age Set to 18 Years. Ratified 7/1/1971.

1. The right of citizens of the United States, who are eighteen years of age or older, to vote shall not be denied or abridged by the United States or by any State on account of age.

2. The Congress shall have power to enforce this article by appropriate legislation.

Amendment 27 - Limiting Changes to Congressional Pay. Ratified 5/7/1992.

No law, varying the compensation for the services of the Senators and Representatives, shall take effect, until an election of Representatives shall have intervened.

THE CONSTITUTION OF THE RUSSIAN FEDERATION

We, the multinational people of the Russian Federation,

united by a common fate on our land,

establishing human rights and freedoms, civic peace and accord,

preserving the historically established state unity,

proceeding from the universally recognized principles of equality and self-determination of peoples,

revering the memory of ancestors who have conveyed to us the love for the Fatherland, belief in the good and justice,

reviving the sovereign statehood of Russia and asserting the firmness of its democratic basic,

striving to ensure the well-being and prosperity of Russia,

proceeding from the responsibility for our Fatherland before the present and future generations, recognizing ourselves as part of the world community,

adopt the CONSTITUTION OF THE RUSSIAN FEDERATION.

FIRST SECTION

CHAPTER 1. THE FUNDAMENTALS OF THE CONSTITUTIONAL SYSTEM

Article 1

The Russian Federation - Russia is a democratic federal law-bound State with a republican form of government.

The names "Russian Federation" and "Russia" shall be equal.

Article 2

Man, his rights and freedoms are the supreme value. The recognition, observance and protection of the rights and freedoms of man and citizen shall be the obligation of the State.

Article 3

1. The bearer of sovereignty and the only source of power in the Russian Federation shall be its multinational people.

2. The people shall exercise their power directly, and also through the bodies of state power and local self-government.

3. The supreme direct expression of the power of the people shall be referenda and free elections.

4. No one may usurp power in the Russian Federation. Seizure of power or usurping state authority shall be prosecuted by federal law.

Article 4

1. The sovereignty of the Russian Federation shall cover the whole of its territory.

2. The Constitution of the Russian Federation and federal laws shall have supremacy in the whole territory of the Russian Federation.

3. The Russian Federation shall ensure the integrity and inviolability of its territory.

Article 5

1. The Russian Federation consists of Republics, territories, regions, cities of federal importance, an autonomous region and autonomous areas - equal subjects of the Russian Federation.

2. The Republic (State) shall have its own constitution and legislation. The territory, region, city of federal importance, autonomous region and autonomous area shall have its charter and legislation.

3. The federal structure of the Russian Federation is based on its state integrity, the unity of the system of state authority, the division of subjects of authority and powers between the bodies of state power of the Russian Federation and bodies of state power of the subjects of the Russian Federation, the equality and self-determination of peoples in the Russian Federation.

4. In relations with federal bodies of state authority all the subjects of the Russian Federation shall be equal among themselves.

Article 6

1. The citizenship of the Russian Federation shall be acquired and terminated according to federal law; it shall be one and equal, irrespective of the grounds of acquisition.

2. Every citizen of the Russian Federation shall enjoy in its territory all the rights and freedoms and bear equal duties provided for by the Constitution of the Russian Federation.

3. A citizen of the Russian Federation may be deprived of his or her citizenship or of the right to change it.

Article 7

1. The Russian Federation is a social State whose policy is aimed at creating conditions for a worthy life and a free development of man.

2. In the Russian Federation the labour and health of people shall be protected, a guaranteed minimum wages and salaries shall be established, state support ensured to the family, maternity, paternity and childhood, to disabled persons and the elderly, the system of social services developed, state pensions, allowances and other social security guarantees shall be established.

Article 8

1. In the Russian Federation guarantees shall be provided for the integrity of economic space, a free flow of goods, services and financial resources, support for competition, and the freedom of economic activity.

2. In the Russian Federation recognition and equal protection shall be given to the private, state, municipal and other forms of ownership.

Article 9

1. Land and other natural resources shall be utilized and protected in the Russian Federation as the

basis of life and activity of the people living in corresponding territories.

2. Land and other natural resources may be in private, state, municipal and other forms of ownership.

Article 10

The state power in the Russian Federation shall be exercised on the basis of its division into legislative, executive and judicial power. The bodies of legislative, executive and judicial power shall be independent.

Article 11

1. The state power in the Russian Federation shall be exercised by the President of the Russian Federation, the Federal Assembly (the Council of the Federation and the State Duma), the Government of the Russian Federation, and the courts of the Russian Federation.

2. The state power in the subjects of the Russian Federation shall be exercised by the bodies of state authority created by them.

3. The division of subjects of authority and power among the bodies of state power of the Russian Federation and the bodies of state power of the subjects of the Russian Federation shall be fixed by the given Constitution, the Federal and other treaties on the delimitation of the subjects of authority and powers.

Article 12

In the Russian Federation local self-government shall be recognized and guaranteed. Local self-government shall be independent within the limits of its authority. The bodies of local self-government shall not be part of the system of bodies of state authority.

Article 13

1. In the Russian Federation ideological diversity shall be recognized.

2. No ideology may be established as state or obligatory one.

3. In the Russian Federation political diversity and multi-party system shall be recognized.

4. Public associations shall be equal before the law.

5. The creation and activities of public associations whose aims and actions are aimed at a forced change of the fundamental principles of the constitutional system and at violating the integrity of the Russian Federation, at undermining its security, at setting up armed units, and at instigating social, racial, national and religious strife shall be prohibited.

Article 14

1. The Russian Federation is a secular state. No religion may be established as a state or obligatory one.

2. Religious associations shall be separated from the State and shall be equal before the law.

Article 15

1. The Constitution of the Russian Federation shall have the supreme juridical force, direct action and shall be used on the whole territory of the Russian Federation. Laws and other legal acts adopted in the Russian Federation shall not contradict the Constitution of the Russian Federation.

2. The bodies of state authority, the bodies of local self-government, officials, private citizens and their associations shall be obliged to observe the Constitution of the Russian Federation and laws.

3. Laws shall be officially published. Unpublished laws shall not be used. Any normative legal acts concerning human rights, freedoms and duties of man and citizen may not be used, if they are not officially published for general knowledge.

4. The universally-recognized norms of international law and international treaties and agreements of the Russian Federation shall be a component part of its legal system. If an international treaty or agreement of the Russian Federation fixes other rules than those envisaged by law, the rules of the international agreement shall be applied.

Article 16

1. The provisions of the present chapter of the Constitution comprise the fundamental principles of the constitutional system of the Russian Federation, and may not be changed otherwise than according to the rules established by the present Constitution.

2. No other provision of the present Constitution may contradict the fundamental principles of the constitutional system of the Russian Federation.

CHAPTER 2. RIGHTS AND FREEDOMS OF MAN AND CITIZEN

Article 17

1. In the Russian Federation recognition and guarantees shall be provided for the rights and freedoms of man and citizen according to the universally recognized principles and norms of international law and according to the present Constitution.

2. Fundamental human rights and freedoms are inalienable and shall be enjoyed by everyone since the day of birth.

3. The exercise of the rights and freedoms of man and citizen shall not violate the rights and freedoms of other people.

Article 18

The rights and freedoms of man and citizen shall be directly operative. They determine the essence, meaning and implementation of laws, the activities of the legislative and executive authorities, local self-government and shall be ensured by the administration of justice.

Article 19

1. All people shall be equal before the law and court.

2. The State shall guarantee the equality of rights and freedoms of man and citizen, regardless of sex, race, nationality, language, origin, property and official status, place of residence, religion, convictions, membership of public associations, and also of other circumstances. All forms of limitations

of human rights on social, racial, national, linguistic or religious grounds shall be banned.

3. Man and woman shall enjoy equal rights and freedoms and have equal possibilities to exercise them.

Article 20

1. Everyone shall have the right to life.

2. Capital punishment until its complete elimination may be envisaged by a federal law as an exclusive penalty for especially grave crimes against life, and the accused shall be granted the right to have his case examined by jurytrial.

Article 21

1. Human dignity shall be protected by the State. Nothing may serve as a basis for its derogation.

2. No one shall be subject to torture, violence or other severe or humiliating treatment or punishment. No one may be subject to medical, scientific and other experiments without voluntary consent.

Article 22

1. Everyone shall have the right to freedom and personal immunity.

2. Arrest, detention and remanding in custody shall be allowed only by court decision. Without the court's decision a person may be detained for a term more than 48 hours.

Article 23

1. Everyone shall have the right to the inviolability of private life, personal and family secrets, the protection of honour and good name.

2. Everyone shall have the right to privacy of correspondence, of telephone conversations, postal, telegraph and other messages. Limitations of this right shall be allowed only by court decision.

Article 24

1. The collection, keeping, use and dissemination of information about the private life of a person shall not be allowed without his or her consent.

2. The bodies of state authority and local self-government, their officials shall ensure for everyone the possibility of acquainting with the documents and materials directly affecting his or her rights and freedoms, unless otherwise provided for by law.

Article 25

The home shall be inviolable. No one shall have the right to get into a house against the will of those living there, except for the cases established by a federal law or by court decision.

Article 26

1. Everyone shall have the right to determine and indicate his nationality. No one may be forced to determine and indicate his or her nationality.

2. Everyone shall have the right to use his or her native language, to a free choice of the language of

communication, upbringing, education and creative work.

Article 27

1. Every who legally stays in the territory of the Russian Federation shall have the right to free travel, choice of place of stay or residence.

2. Everyone may freely leave the Russian Federation. Citizens of the Russian Federation shall have the right to freely return to the Russian Federation.

Article 28

Everyone shall be guaranteed the freedom of conscience, the freedom of religion, including the right to profess individually or together with other any religion or to profess no religion at all, to freely choose, possess and disseminate religious and other views and act according to them.

Article 29

1. Everyone shall be guaranteed the freedom of ideas and speech.

2. The propaganda or agitation instigating social, racial, national or religious hatred and strife shall not be allowed. The propaganda of social, racial, national, religious or linguistic supremacy shall be banned.

3. No one may be forced to express his views and convictions or to reject them.

4. Everyone shall have the right to freely look for, receive, transmit, produce and distribute information by any legal way. The list of data comprising state secrets shall be determined by a federal law.

5. The freedom of mass communication shall be guaranteed. Censorship shall be banned.

Article 30

1. Everyone shall have the right to association, including the right to create trade unions for the protection of his or her interests. The freedom of activity of public association shall be guaranteed.

2. No one may be compelled to join any association and remain in it.

Article 31

Citizens of the Russian Federation shall have the right to assemble peacefully, without weapons, hold rallies, meetings and demonstrations, marches and pickets.

Article 32

1. Citizens of the Russian Federation shall have the right to participate in managing state affairs both directly and through their representatives.

2. Citizens of the Russian Federation shall have the right to elect and be elected to state bodies of power and local self-government bodies, and also to participate in referenda.

3. Deprived of the right to elect and be elected shall be citizens recognized by court as legally unfit, as well as citizens kept in places of confinement by a court sentence.

4. Citizens of the Russian Federation shall enjoy equal access to the state service.

5. Citizens of the expenditures shall have the right to participate in administering justice.

Article 33

Citizens of the Russian Federation shall have the right to address personally, as well as to submit individual and collective appeals to state organs and local self-government bodies.

Article 34

1. Everyone shall have the right to a free use of his abilities and property for entrepreneurial and economic activities not prohibited by law.

2. The economic activity aimed at monopolization and unfair competition shall not be allowed.

Article 35

1. The right of private property shall be protected by law.

2. Everyone shall have the right to have property, possess, use and dispose of it both personally and jointly with other people.

3. No one may be deprived of property otherwise than by a court decision. Forced confiscation of property for state needs may be carried out only on the proviso of preliminary and complete compensation.

4. The right of inheritance shall be guaranteed.

Article 36

1. Citizens and their associations shall have the right to possess land as private property.

2. Possession, utilization and disposal of land and other natural resources shall be exercised by the owners freely, if it is not detrimental to the environment and does not violate the rights and lawful interests of other people.

3. The terms and rules for the use of land shall be fixed by a federal law.

Article 37

1. Labour is free. Everyone shall have the right to freely use his labour capabilities, to choose the type of activity and profession.

2. Forced labour shall be banned.

3. Everyone shall have the right to labour conditions meeting the safety and hygienic requirements, for labour remuneration without any discrimination whatsoever and not lower than minimum wages and salaries established by the federal law, as well as the right to protection against unemployment.

4. Recognition shall be given to the right to individual and collective labour disputes with the use of methods of their adjustment fixed by the federal law, including the right to strike.

5. Everyone shall have the right to rest and license. Those working by labour contracts shall be guaranteed the fixed duration of the working time, days off and holidays, and the annual paid leave established by the federal law.

Article 38

1. Maternity and childhood, and the family shall be protected by the State.

2. Care for children, their upbringing shall be equally the right and obligation of parents.

3. Able-bodied children over 18 years of age shall take care of disabled parents.

Article 39

1. Everyone shall be guaranteed social security at the expense of the State in old age, in case of an illness, disableness, loss of the bread-winner, for upbringing of children and in other cases established by law.

2. State pensions and social allowances shall be established by law.

3. Promotion shall be given to voluntary social insurance and the creation of additional forms of social security and charity.

Article 40

1. Everyone shall have the right to a home. No one may be arbitrarily deprived of his or her home.

2. The bodies of state authority and local self-government shall encourage housing construction and create conditions for exercising the right to a home.

3. Low-income people and other persons mentioned in law and in need of a home shall receive it gratis or for reasonable payment from the state, municipal and other housing stocks according to the norms fixed by law.

Article 41

1. Everyone shall have the right to health protection and medical aid. Medical aid in state and municipal health establishments shall be rendered to individuals gratis, at the expense of the corresponding budget, insurance contributions, and other proceeds.

2. In the Russian Federation federal programmes of protecting and strengthening the health of the population shall be financed by the State; measures shall be adopted to develop state, municipal and

private health services; activities shall be promoted which facilitate the strengthening of health, the development of physical culture and sport, ecological and sanitary-epidemiological well-being.

3. The concealment by officials of the facts and circumstances posing a threat to the life and health of people shall entail responsibility according to the federal law.

Article 42

Everyone shall have the right to favourable environment, reliable information about its state and for a restitution of damage inflicted on his health and property by ecological transgressions.

Article 43

1. Everyone shall have the right to education.

2. Guarantees shall be provided for general access to and free pre-school, secondary and high vocational education in state or municipal educational establishments and at enterprises.

3. Everyone shall have the right to receive on a competitive basis a free higher education in a state or municipal educational establishment and at an enterprise.

4. The basic general education shall be free of charge. Parents or persons in law parents shall enable their children to receive a basic general education.

5. The Russian Federation shall establish federal state educational standards and support various forms of education and self-education.

1. Everyone shall be guaranteed the freedom of literary, artistic, scientific, technical and other types of creative activity, and teaching. Intellectual property shall be protected by law.

2. Everyone shall have the right to participate in cultural life and use cultural establishments and to an access to cultural values.

3. Everyone shall be obliged to care for the preservation of cultural and historical heritage and protect monuments of history and culture.

Article 45

1. State protection of the rights and freedoms of man and citizen shall be guaranteed in the Russian Federation.

2. Everyone shall be free to protect his rights and freedoms by all means not prohibited by law.

Article 46

1. Everyone shall be guaranteed judicial protection of his rights and freedoms.

2. Decisions and actions (or inaction) of bodies of state authority and local self-government, public associations and officials may be appealed against in court.

3. Everyone shall have the right to appeal, according to international treaties of the Russian Federation, to international bodies for the protection of human rights and freedoms, if all the existing internal state means of legal protection have been exhausted.

Article 47

1. No one may be deprived of the right to the consideration of his or her case in that court and by that judge in whose cognizance the given case is according to law.

2. The accused of committing a crime shall have the right to the examination of his case by a court of jury in cases envisaged by the federal law.

Article 48

1. Everyone shall be guaranteed the right to qualified legal assistance. In cases envisaged by law the legal assistance shall be free.

2. Any person detained, taken into custody, accused of committing a crime shall have the right to receive assistance of a lawyer (counsel for the defence) from the moment of detention, confinement in custody or facing charges accordingly.

Article 49

1. Everyone accused of committing a crime shall be considered innocent until his guilt is proved according to the rules fixed by the federal law and confirmed by the sentence of a court which has come into legal force.

2. The accused shall not be obliged to prove his innocence.

3. Unremovable doubts about the guilt of a person shall be interpreted in favour of the accused.

Article 50

1. No one may be convicted twice for one and the same crime.

2. In administering justice it shall not be allowed to use evidence received by violating the federal law.

3. Everyone convicted for a crime shall have the right to appeal against the judgement of a superior court according to the rules envisaged by the federal law, as well as to ask for pardon or a mitigation of punishment.

Article 51

1. No one shall be obliged to give incriminating evidence, husband or wife and close relatives the range of whom is determined by the federal law.

2. The federal law may envisage other cases of absolution from the obligation to testify.

Article 52

The rights of victims of crimes and of abuse of office shall be protected by law. The State shall provide access to justice for them and a compensation for sustained damage.

Article 53

Everyone shall have the right for a state compensation for damages caused by unlawful actions (inaction) of bodies of state authority and their officials.

Article 54

1. A law introducing or aggravating responsibility shall not have retrospective effect.

2. No one may bear responsibility for the action which was not regarded as a crime when it was committed. If after violating law the responsibility for that is eliminated or mitigated, a new law shall be applied.

Article 55

1. The listing in the Constitution of the Russian Federation of the fundamental rights and freedoms shall not be interpreted as a rejection or derogation of other universally recognized human rights and freedoms.

2. In the Russian Federation no laws shall be adopted cancelling or derogating human rights and freedoms.

3. The rights and freedoms of man and citizen may be limited by the federal law only to such an extent to which it is necessary for the protection of the fundamental principles of the constitutional system, morality, health, the rights and lawful interests of

other people, for ensuring defence of the country and security of the State.

Article 56

1. In conditions of a state of emergency in order to ensure the safety of citizens and the protection of the constitutional system and in accordance with the federal constitutional law certain limitations may be placed on human rights and freedoms with the establishment of their framework and time period.

2. A state of emergency may be introduced in the whole territory of the Russian Federation and in its certain parts in case there are circumstances and according to the rules fixed by the federal constitutional law.

3. The rights and freedoms envisaged in Articles 20, 21, 23 (the first part), 24, 28, 34 (the first part), 40 (the first part), 46-54 of the Constitution of the Russian Federation, shall not be liable to limitations.

Article 57

Everyone shall be obliged to pay the legally established taxes and dues. Laws introducing new taxes or deteriorating the position of taxpayers may not have retroactive effect.

Article 58

Everyone shall be obliged to preserve nature and the environment, carefully treat the natural wealth.

Article 59

1. Defence of the Fatherland shall be a duty and obligation of citizens of the Russian Federation.

2. A citizen shall carry out military service according to the federal law.

3. A citizen of the Russian Federation shall have the right to replace military service by alternative civilian service in case his convictions or religious belief contradict military service and also in other cases envisaged by the federal law.

Article 60

A citizen of the Russian Federation may exercise his or her rights and duties in full from the age of 18.

Article 61

1. A citizen of the Russian Federation may not be deported from Russia or extradited to another State.

2. The Russian Federation shall guarantee to its citizens protection and patronage abroad.

Article 62

1. A citizen of the Russian Federation may have the citizenship of a foreign State (dual citizenship) according to the federal law or an international agreement of the Russian Federation.

2. The possession of a foreign citizenship by a citizen of the Russian Federation shall not derogate

his rights and freedoms and shall not free him from the obligations stipulated by the Russian citizenship, unless otherwise provided for by federal law or an international agreement of the Russian Federation.

3. Foreign nationals and stateless persons shall enjoy in the Russian Federation the rights and bear the obligations of citizens of the Russian Federation, except for cases envisaged by the federal law or the international agreement of the Russian Federation.

Article 63

1. The Russian Federation shall grant political asylum to foreign nationals and stateless persons according to the universally recognized norms of international law.

2. In the Russian Federation it shall not be allowed to extradite to other States those people who are persecuted for political convictions, as well as for actions (or inaction) not recognized as a crime in the Russian Federation. The extradition of people accused of a crime, and also the handover of convicts for serving sentences in other States shall be carried out on the basis of the federal law or the international agreement of the Russian Federation.

Article 64

The provisions of the present chapter comprise the basis of the legal status of the individual in the Russian Federation and may not be changed otherwise then according to the rules introduced by the present Constitution.

CHAPTER 3. THE FEDERAL STRUCTURE

Article 65

1. The Russian Federation includes the following subjects of the Russian Federation:

the Republic of Adygeya (Adygeya), the Republic of Altai, the Republic of Bashkortostan, the Republic of Buryatia, the Republic of Daghestan, the Republic of Ingushetia, the Kabardino-Balkarian Republic, the Republic of Kalmykia, the Karachayevo-Circassian Republic, the Republic of Karelia, the Komi Republic, the Republic of Marii El, the Republic of Mordovia, the Republic of Sakha (Yakutia), the Republic of North Ossetia - Alania, the

Republic of Tatarstan (Tatarstan), the Republic of Tuva, the Udmurtian Republic, the Republic of Khakassia, the Chechen Republic, the Chuvash Republic - Chuvashia;

the Altai Territory, the Krasnodar Territory, the Krasnoyarsk Territory, the Primorie Territory, the Stavropol Territory, the Khabarovsk Territory;

the Amur Region, the Archangel Region, the Astrakhan Region, the Belgorod Region, the Bryansk Region, the Vladimir Region, the Volgograd Region, the Vologda Region, the Voronezh Region, the Ivanovo Region, the Irkutsk Region, the Kaliningrad Region, the Kaluga Region, the Kamchatka Region, the Kemerovo Region, the Kirov Region, the Kostroma Region, the Kurgan Region, the Kursk Region, the Leningrad Region, the Lipetsk Region, the Magadan Region, the Moscow Region, the Murmansk Region, the Nizhni Novgorod Region, the Novgorod Region, the Novosibirsk Region, the Omsk Region, the Orenburg Region, the Orel Region, the Penza Region, the Perm Region, the Pskov Region, the Rostov Region, the Ryazan Region, the Samara Region, the Saratov Region, the Sakhalin Region, the Sverdlovsk Region, the Smolensk Region, the Tambov Region, the Tver Region, the Tomsk Region, the Tula Region, the Tyumen Region, the Ulyanovsk Region, the Chelyabinsk Region, the Chita Region, the Yaroslavl Region;

Moscow, St. Petersburg - cities of federal importance;

the Jewish Autonomous Region;

the Aginsk Buryat Autonomous Area, the Komi-Permyak Autonomous Area, the Koryak Autonomous Area, the Nenets Autonomous Area, the Taimyr (Dolgano-Nenets) Autonomous Area, the Ust-Ordyn Buryat Autonomous Area, the Khanty-Mansi Autonomous Area, the Chukotka Autonomous Area, the Evenki Autonomous Area, the Yamalo-Nents Autonomous Area.

2. The admission to the Russian Federation and the creation in it of a new subject shall be carried out according to the rules established by the federal constitutional law.

Article 66

1. The status of a Republic shall be determined by the Constitution of the Russian Federation and the Constitution of the Republic.

2. The status of a territory, region, city of federal importance, autonomous region and autonomous area shall be determined by the Constitution of the Russian Federation and the Charter of the territory, region,

city of federal importance, autonomous region or autonomous area, adopted by the legislative (representative) body of the corresponding subject of the Russian Federation.

3. Upon the proposal of the legislative and executive bodies of the autonomous region or autonomous area a federal law on autonomous region or autonomous area may be adopted.

4. The relations between the autonomous area within a territory or region may be regulated by the federal law or a treaty between the bodies of state authority of the autonomous area and, accordingly, the bodies of state authority of the territory or region.

5. The status of a subject of the Russian Federation may be changed upon mutual agreement of the Russian Federation and the subject of the Russian Federation and according to the federal constitutional law.

Article 67

1. The territory of the Russian Federation shall include the territories of its subjects, inland waters and territorial sea, and the air space over them.

2. The Russian Federation shall possess sovereign rights and exercise the jurisdiction on the continental shelf and in the exclusive economic zone of the Russian Federation according to the rules fixed by the federal law and the norms of international law.

3. The borders between the subjects of the Russian Federation may be changed upon their mutual consent.

Article 68

1. The Russian language shall be a state language on the whole territory of the Russian Federation.

2. The Republics shall have the right to establish their own state languages. In the bodies of state authority and local self-government, state institutions of the Republics they shall be used together with the state language of the Russian Federation.

3. The Russian Federation shall guarantee to all of its peoples the right to preserve their native language and to create conditions for its study and development.

Article 69

The Russian Federation shall guarantee the rights of the indigenous small peoples according to the universally recognized principles and norms of international law and international treaties and agreements of the Russian Federation.

Article 70

1. The state flag, coat of arms and anthem of the Russian Federation, their description and rules of official use shall be established by the federal constitutional law.

The capital of the Russian Federation is the city of Moscow. The status of the capital shall be determined by the federal law.

Article 71

The jurisdiction of the Russian Federation includes:

a) adoption and amending of the Constitution of the Russian Federation and federal laws, control over their observance;

b) federal structure and the territory of the Russian Federation;

c) regulation and protection of the rights and freedoms of man and citizen; citizenship in the Russian Federation, regulation and protection of the rights of national minorities;

d) establishment of the system of federal bodies of legislative, executive and judicial authority, the rules of their organization and activities, formation of federal bodies of state authority;

e) federal state property and its management;

f) establishment of the principles of federal policy and federal programmes in the sphere of state, economic, ecological, social, cultural and national development of the Russian Federation;

g) establishment of legal groups for a single market; financial, currency, credit, and customs regulation, money issue, the principles of pricing policy; federal economic services, including federal banks;

h) federal budget, federal taxes and dues, federal funds of regional development;

i) federal power systems, nuclear power-engineering, fission materials, federal transport, railways, information and communication, outer space activities;

j) foreign policy and international relations of the Russian Federation, international treaties and agreements of the Russian Federation, issues of war and peace;

k) foreign economic relations of the Russian Federation;

l) defence and security; military production; determination of rules of selling and purchasing weapons, ammunition, military equipment and other military property; production of poisonous substances, narcotic substances and rules of their use;

m) determination of the status and protection of the state border, territorial sea, air space, exclusive economic zone and continental shelf of the expenditures;

n) judicial system, procurator's office, criminal, criminal procedure and criminal-executive legislation, amnesty and pardoning , civil, civil procedure and arbitration procedure legislation, legal regulation of intellectual property;

o) federal law of conflict of laws;

p) meteorological service, standards, metric system, horometry accounting, geodesy and cartography, names of geographical units, official statistics and accounting;

q) state awards and honourary titles of the Russian Federation;

r) federal state service.

Article 72

1. The joint jurisdiction of the Russian Federation and the subjects of the Russian Federation includes:

a) providing for the correspondence of the constitutions and laws of the Republics, the charters and other normative legal acts of the territories, regions, cities of federal importance, autonomous regions or autonomous areas to the Constitution of the Russian Federation and the federal laws;

b) protection of the rights and freedoms of man and citizen; protection of the rights of national minorities; ensuring the rule of law, law and order, public security, border zone regime;

c) issues of possession, use and disposal of land, subsoil, water and other natural resources;

d) delimitation of state property;

e) nature utilization, protection of the environment and ensuring ecological safety; specially protected natural territories, protection of historical and cultural monuments;

f) general issues of upbringing, education, science, culture, physical culture and sports;

g) coordination of issues of health care; protection of the family, maternity, paternity and childhood; social protection, including social security;

h) carrying out measures against catastrophes, natural calamities, epidemics, elimination of their aftermath;

i) establishment of common principles of taxation and dues in the Russian Federation;

j) administrative, administrative procedure, labour, family, housing, land, water, and forest legislation; legislation on subsoil and environmental protection;

k) personnel of the judicial and law enforcement agencies; the Bar, notaryship;

l) protection of traditional living habitat and of traditional way of life of small ethnic communities;

m) establishment of common principles of organization of the system of bodies of state authority and local self-government;

n) coordination of international and foreign economic relations of the subjects of the Russian Federation, fulfillment of international treaties and agreements of the Russian Federation.

2. Provisions of this Article shall be equally valid for the Republics, territories, regions, cities of federal importance, autonomous regions or autonomous areas.

Article 73

Outside the limits of authority of the Russian Federation and the powers of the Russian Federation on issues under joint jurisdiction of the Russian Federation and the subjects of the Russian Federation, the subjects of the Russian Federation shall possess full state power.

Article 74

1. In the territory of the Russian Federation it shall not be allowed to establish customs borders, dues or any other barriers for a free flow of goods, services and financial resources.

2. Limitations on the transfer of goods and services may be introduced according to the federal law, if it is necessary to ensure security, protect the life and health of people, protect nature and cultural values.

Article 75

1. The monetary unit in the Russian Federation shall be the rouble. Money issue shall be carried out exclusively by the Central Bank of the Russian Federation. Introduction and issue of other currencies in Russia shall not be allowed.

2. The protection and ensuring the stability of the rouble shall be the major task of the Central Bank

of the Russian Federation, which it shall fulfil independently of the other bodies of state authority.

3. The system of taxes paid to the federal budget and the general principles of taxation and dues in the Russian Federation shall be fixed by the federal law.

4. State loans shall be issued according to the rules fixed by the federal law and shall be floated on a voluntary basis.

Article 76

1. On the issues under the jurisdiction of the Russian Federation federal constitutional laws and federal laws shall be adopted and have direct action in the whole territory of the Russian Federation.

2. On the issues under the joint jurisdiction of the Russian Federation and subjects of the Russian Federation federal laws shall issued and laws and other normative acts of the subjects of the Russian Federation shall be adopted according to them.

3. Federal laws may not contradict the federal constitutional laws.

4. Outside the limits of authority of the Russian Federation, of the joint jurisdiction of the Russian

Federation and the subjects of the Russian Federation, the Republics, territories, regions, cities of federal importance, autonomous regions or autonomous areas shall exercise their own legal regulation, including the adoption of laws and other normative acts.

5. The laws and other legislative acts of the subjects of the Russian Federation may not contradict the federal laws adopted according to the first and second parts of this Article. In case of a contradiction between a federal law and an act issued in the Russian Federation the federal law shall be applied.

6. In case of a contradiction between a federal law and a normative act of a subject of the Russian Federation adopted according to the fourth part of this Article, the normative legal act of the subject of the Russian Federation shall be applied.

Article 77

1. The system of bodies of state authority of the Republics, territories, regions, cities of federal importance, autonomous regions or autonomous areas shall be established by the subjects of the Russian Federation independently and according to the principles of the constitutional system of the Russian Federation and the general principles of the

organization of representative and executive bodies of state authority fixed by federal law.

2. Within the limits of jurisdiction of the Russian Federation and the powers of the Russian Federation on the issue under the joint jurisdiction of the Russian Federation and the subjects of the Russian Federation the federal bodies of executive authority and the bodies of executive authority of the subjects of the Russian Federation shall make up a single system of executive power of the Russian Federation.

Article 78

1. The federal bodies of executive power in order to exercise their powers may create their own territorial organs and appoint corresponding officials.

2. The federal bodies of executive power by agreement with the bodies of executive power of the subjects of the Russian Federation may transfer to them the fulfillment of a part of their powers, if it does not contradict the Constitution of the Russian Federation and the federal laws.

3. The bodies of executive power of the subjects of the Russian Federation by agreement with the federal bodies of executive authority may transfer to them the fulfillment of a part of their powers.

4. The President of the Russian Federation and the Government of the Russian Federation shall ensure, according to the Constitution of the Russian Federation, the implementation of the powers of the federal state authority in the whole territory of the Russian Federation.

Article 79

The Russian Federation may participate in interstate associations and transfer to them part of its powers according to international treaties and agreements, if this does not involve the limitation of the rights and freedoms of man and citizen and does not contradict the principles of the constitutional system of the Russian Federation.

CHAPTER 4. THE PRESIDENT OF THE RUSSIAN FEDERATION

Article 80

1. The President of the Russian Federation shall be the head of the State.

2. The President of the Russian Federation shall be guarantor of the Constitution of the Russian Federation, of the rights and freedoms of man and citizen. According to the rules fixed by the Constitution of the Russian Federation, he shall adopt measures to protect the sovereignty of the Russian Federation, its independence and state integrity, ensure coordinated functioning and interaction of all the bodies of state power.

3. According to the Constitution of the Russian Federation and the federal laws the President of the Russian Federation shall determine the guidelines of the internal and foreign policies of the State.

4. As the head of the State the President of the Russian Federation represent the Russian Federation within the country and in international relations.

Article 81

1. The President of the Russian Federation shall be elected for four years by citizens of the Russian

Federation on the basis of universal, equal, direct suffrage by secret ballot.

2. Any citizen of the Russian Federation not younger than 35 years of age and with a permanent residence record in the Russian Federation of not less than 10 years may be elected President of the Russian Federation.

3. One and the same person may not be elected President of the Russian Federation for more than two terms running.

4. The rules of electing the President of the Russian Federation shall determined by the federal law.

Article 82

1. When taking office the President of the Russian Federation shall take the following oath of loyalty to the people:

"I swear in exercising the powers of the President of the Russian Federation to respect and safeguard the rights and freedoms of man and citizen, to observe and protect the Constitution of the Russian Federation, to protect the sovereignty and independence, security and integrity of the State, to faithfully serve the people".

2. The oath shall be taken in a solemn atmosphere in the presence of members of the Council of the Federation, deputies of the State Duma and judges of the Constitution Court of the Russian Federation.

Article 83

The President of the Russian Federation shall:

a) appoint by agreement with the State Duma the Chairman of the Government of the Russian Federation;

b) have the right to chair meetings of the Government of the Russian Federation;

c) adopt decision on the registration of the Government of the Russian Federation;

d) present to the State Duma a candidate for the appointment to the post of the Chairman of the Central Bank of the Russian Federation, raise before the State Duma the issue of dismissing the Chairman of the Central Bank of the Russian Federation;

e) on the proposal by the Chairman of the Government of the Russian Federation appoint and dismiss deputy chairmen of the Government of the Russian Federation and federal ministers;

f) present to the Council of the Federation candidates for appointment as judges of the Constitution Court of the Russian Federation, the Supreme Court of the Russian Federation, the Higher Court of Arbitration of the Russian Federation, as well as a candidate for the post of the Procurator-General of the Russian Federation; appoint judges of other federal courts;

g) form and head the Security Council of the Russian Federation, the status of which is determined by the federal law;

h) approve the military doctrine of the Russian Federation;

i) form the Administration of the President of the Russian Federation;

j) appoint and dismiss plenipotentiary representatives of the President of the Russian Federation;

k) appoint and dismiss the supreme command of the Armed Forces of the Russian Federation;

l) after consultations with corresponding committees and commissions of the chambers of the

Federal Assembly appoint and recall diplomatic representatives of the Russian Federation in foreign States and international organizations.

Article 84

The President of the Russian Federation shall:

a) announce elections to the State Duma according to the Constitution of the Russian Federation and the federal law;

b) dissolve the State Duma in cases and according to the rules fixed by the Constitution of the Russian Federation;

c) announce a referendum according to the rules fixed by the federal constitutional law;

d) submit bills to the State Duma;

e) sign and make public the federal laws;

f) address the Federal Assembly with annual messages on the situation in the country, on the guidelines of the internal and foreign policy of the State.

Article 85

1. The President of the Russian Federation may use conciliatory procedures to solve disputes between the bodies of state authority of the Russian Federation and bodies of state authority of the subjects of the Russian Federation, as well as between bodies of state authority of the subjects of the Russian Federation. In case no agreed decision is reached, he shall have the right to submit the dispute for the consideration of a corresponding court.

2. The President of the Russian Federation shall have the right to suspend acts of the Bodies of executive power of the subjects of the Russian Federation in case these acts contradict the Constitution of the Russian Federation and the federal laws, international commitments of the Russian Federation or violate the rights and freedoms of man and citizen until the issue is solved by a corresponding court.

Article 86

The President of the Russian Federation shall:

a) govern the foreign policy of the Russian Federation;

b) hold negotiations and sign international treaties and agreements of the Russian Federation;

c) sign ratification instruments;

d) received credentials and letters of recall of diplomatic representatives accredited to him.

Article 87

1. The President of the Russian Federation shall be the Supreme Commander-in-Chief of the Armed Forces of the Russian Federation.

2. In case of an aggression against the Russian Federation or of a direct threat of aggression the President of the Russian Federation shall introduce in the territory of the Russian Federation or in its certain parts a martial law and immediately inform the Council of the Federation and the State Duma about this .

3. The regime of the martial law shall be defined by the federal constitutional law.

Article 88

The President of the Russian Federation, in circumstances and according to the rules envisaged by the federal constitutional law, shall introduce a state of emergency in the territory of the Russian Federation or in its certain parts and immediately inform the Council of the Federation and the State Duma about this.

Article 89

The President of the Russian Federation shall:

a) solve the issues of citizenship of the Russian Federation and of granting political asylum;

b) decorate with state awards of the Russian Federation, award honourary titles of the Russian Federation, higher military and higher special ranks;

c) decide on pardoning.

Article 90

1. The President of the Russian Federation shall issue decrees and orders.

2. The decrees and orders of the President of the Russian Federation shall be obligatory for fulfillment in the whole territory of the Russian Federation.

3. Decrees and orders of the President of the Russian Federation shall not run counter to the Constitution of the Russian Federation and the federal laws.

Article 91

The President of the Russian Federation shall possess immunity.

Article 92

1. The President of the Russian Federation shall take up his powers since the moment of taking the oath of loyalty and cease to fulfil them with the expiration of the term of office and from the moment a newly-elected president is sworn in.

2. The President of the Russian Federation shall cease to exercise his powers short of the term in case of his resignation, stable inability because of health reasons to exercise the powers vested in him or in case of impeachment. In this case the election of the President of the Russian Federation shall take place not later than three months since the termination of the powers short of the term.

3. In all cases when the President of the Russian Federation is incapable of fulfilling his duties, they shall temporarily fulfilled by the Chairman of the Government of the Russian Federation. The Acting President of the Russian Federation shall have no right to dissolve the State Duma, appoint a referendum, and also provisions of the Constitution of the Russian Federation.

Article 93

1. The President of the Russian Federation may be impeached by the Council of the Federation only on the basis of the charges of high treason or another grave crime, advanced by the State Duma and confirmed by the conclusion of the Supreme Court of the Russian Federation on the presence of the elements of crime in the actions of the President of

the Russian Federation and by the conclusion of the Constitution Court of the Russian Federation confirming that the rules of advancing the charges were observed.

2. The decision of the State Duma on advancing charges and the decision of the Council of the Federation on impeaching the President shall be adopted by two thirds of the votes of the total number of members of each chamber and on the initiative of not less than one third of the deputies of the State Duma and with the conclusion of a special commission set up by the State Duma.

3. The decision of the Council of the Federation on impeaching the President of the Russian Federation shall be adopted not later than three months after the State Duma advanced the charges against the President. If a decision of the Council of the Federation is not adopted during this time, the charges against the President shall be regarded as rejected.

CHAPTER 5. THE FEDERAL ASSEMBLY

Article 94

The Federal Assembly - the parliament of the Russian Federation - shall be the representative and legislative body of the Russian Federation.

Article 95

1. The Federal Assembly consists of two chambers - the Council of the Federation and the State Duma.

2. The Council of the Federation includes two representatives from each subject of the Russian Federation: one from the legislative and one from the executive body of state authority.

3. The State Duma consists of 450 deputies.

Article 96

1. The State Duma shall be elected for a term of four years.

2. The rules of forming the Council of the Federation and the rules of electing deputies to the State Duma shall be introduced federal laws.

Article 97

1. A citizen of the Russian Federation over 21 years of age and with the right to participate in elections may be elected deputy of the State Duma.

2. One and the same person may not be simultaneously a member of the Council of the Federation and a deputy of the State Duma. A deputy of the State Duma may not be a deputy of other representative bodies of state authority and local self-government.

3. Deputies of the State Duma shall work on a permanent professional basis. Deputies of the State Duma may not be employed in the state service, engage in other paid activities, except for teaching, scientific and other creative work.

Article 98

1. Members of the Council of the Federation and deputies of the State Duma shall possess immunity during the whole term of their mandate. They may not be detained, arrested, searched, except for cases of

detention at the site of crime. They may not be personally inspected, except for the cases envisaged by the federal law in order to ensure the safety of other people.

2. The issue of depriving immunity shall be solved upon the proposal of the Procurator General of the Russian Federation to the corresponding chamber of the Federal Assembly.

Article 99

1. The Federal Assembly shall work on a permanent basis.

2. The State Duma shall be convened at its first sitting on the thirtieth day after the elections. The President of the Russian Federation may convene a sitting of the State Duma earlier then the mentioned time.

3. The first sitting of the State Duma shall be opened by the oldest deputy.

4. Since the time the State Duma of a new convocation begins to work the mandate of the State Duma of the previous convocation shall expire.

Article 100

1. The Council of the Federation and the State Duma shall hold separate sittings.

2. Sittings of the Council of the Federation and of the State Duma shall open. In cases envisaged by procedural rules the chambers shall have the right to hold closed-door sittings.

3. The chambers may hold joint sittings for the consideration of the messages of the President of the Russian Federation, the messages of the Constitution Court of the Russian Federation, and speeches of leaders of foreign states.

Article 101

1. The Council of the Federation shall elect from among its deputies the Chairman of the Council of the Federation and his deputies. The State Duma shall elect from among its deputies the Chairman of the State Duma and his deputies.

2. The Chairman of the Council of the Federation and his deputes, the Chairman of the State Duma and his deputies chair sittings and shall be in

charge of the internal routine work of the respective chamber.

3. The Council of the Federation and the State Duma shall set up committees and commissions, hold parliamentary hearings on issues in their authority.

4. Each of the chambers shall adopt its procedural rules and solve issues of procedure for its work.

5. For controlling the implementation of the federal budget the Council of the Federation and the State Duma shall create the Accounting Chamber, the composition and the rules of work of which are fixed by the federal law.

Article 102

1. The jurisdiction of the Council of the Federation includes:

a) approval of changes in borders between subjects of the Russian Federation;

b) approval of the decree of the President of the Russian Federation on the introduction of a martial law;

c) approval of the decree of the President of the Russian Federation on the introduction of a state of emergency;

d) deciding on the possibility of using the Armed Forces of the Russian Federation outside the territory of the Russian Federation;

e) appointment of elections of the President of the Russian Federation;

f) impeachment of the President of the Russian Federation;

g) appointment of judges of the Constitution Court of the Russian Federation, of the Supreme Court of the Russian Federation, of the Higher Arbitration Court of the Russian Federation;

h) appointment and dismissal of the Procurator-General of the Russian Federation;

i) appointment and dismissal of Deputy Chairman and half of the auditors of the all Accounting Chamber.

2. The Council of the Federation shall adopt resolutions on the issues referred to its authority by the Constitution of the Russian Federation.

3. Resolution of the Council of the Federation shall be adopted by a majority of the total number of the members of the Council of the Federation, if other

rules for adopting decisions are not envisaged by the Constitution of the Russian Federation.

Article 103

1. The jurisdiction of the State Duma includes:

a) approving the appointment of the Chairman of the Government of the Russian Federation by the President of the Russian Federation;

b) solution of the issue of confidence in the Government of the Russian Federation;

c) appointment and dismissal of the Chairman of the Central Bank of the Russian Federation;

d) appointment and dismissal of the Chairman and half of the auditors of the Accounting Chamber;

e) appointment and dismissal of the Commissioner for human rights, who acts according to the federal constitutional law;

f) proclamation of amnesty;

g) advancing of charges against the President of the Russian Federation for his impeachment.

2. The State Duma shall adopt resolutions on the issues referred to its authority by the Constitution of the Russian Federation.

3. Resolutions of the State Duma shall be adopted by a majority of the total number of the deputies of the State Duma, if other rules for adopting decisions are not stipulated by the Constitution of the Russian Federation.

Article 104

1. The power to initiate legislation shall belong to the President of the Russian Federation, the Council of the Federation, the members of the Council of the Federation, the deputies of the State Duma, the Government of the Russian Federation, and the legislative (representative) bodies of the subjects of the Russian Federation. The power to initiate legislation shall also belong to the Constitution Court of the Russian Federation, the Supreme Court of the Russian Federation, the Higher Arbitration Court of the Russian Federation on the issues in their authority.

2. Bills shall be submitted to the State Duma.

3. Bills on the introduction or cancellation of taxes, on exemption from their payment, on the issue of state loans, on changes in the financial obligations of the State, and other bills envisaging expenses covered from the federal budget may be submitted only upon the conclusion of the Government of the Russian Federation.

Article 105

1. Federal laws shall be adopted by the State Duma.

2. Federal laws shall be adopted by a majority of votes of the total number of the deputies of the State Duma, unless otherwise envisaged by the Constitution of the Russian Federation.

3. The federal laws adopted by the State Duma shall be submitted in five days for the consideration of the Council of the Federation.

4. A federal law shall be considered to be approved by the Council of the Federation, if over a half of the total number of the members of the chamber have voted for it or if the Council of the Federation does not consider it in fourteen days. In

case the Council of the Federation rejects a law, the chambers may create a conciliatory commission for overcoming the contradictions that arose, after which the federal law shall be recognized by the State Duma.

5. In case the State Duma disagrees with the decision of the Council of the Federation, a federal law shall be considered adopted, if during the second vote not less than two thirds of the total number of the deputies of the State Duma supported it.

Article 106

Liable to obligatory consideration by the Council of the Federation shall be the federal laws adopted by the State Duma on the following issues:

a) federal budget;

b) federal taxes and dues;

c) financial, currency, credit, customs regulation, and money issue;

d) ratification and denunciation of international treaties and agreements of the Russian Federation;

e) the status and protection of the state border of the Russian Federation;

f) peace and war.

Article 107

1. The adopted federal law shall be submitted in five days to the President of the Russian Federation for signing and making it public.

2. The President of the Russian Federation shall sign the federal law and make it public in fourteen days.

3. If in fourteen days since the moment of receiving the federal law the President rejects it, the State Duma and the Council of the Federation shall reconsider the given law according to the rules fixed by the Constitution of the Russian Federation. If during the second vote the law is approved in the earlier adopted wording by not less than two thirds of the total number of the members of the Council of the Federation and of the deputies of the State Duma, it shall be signed by the President in seven days and made public.

Article 108

1. Federal constitutional laws shall be adopted on the issues envisaged by the Constitution of the Russian Federation.

2. A federal constitutional law shall be considered to be adopted, if it is approved by not less than three fourths of the total number of the members of the Council of the Federation and not less than two thirds of the total number of the deputies of the State Duma. The adopted federal constitutional law shall be signed by the President of the Russian Federation in fourteen days and made public.

Article 109

1. The State Duma may be dissolved by the President of the Russian Federation in cases envisaged in Articles 111 and 117 of the Constitution of the Russian Federation.

2. In case the State Duma is dissolved, the President of the Russian Federation shall appoint the

date of election so that a newly-elected State Duma could meet not later than four months since the moment of dissolution.

3. The State Duma may not be dissolved on the grounds envisaged in Article 117 of the Constitution of the Russian Federation during a year after it was elected.

4. The State Duma may not be dissolved from the moment it advances charges against the President of the Russian Federation until the Council of the Federation adopts a decision on the issue.

5. The State Duma may not be dissolved while a state of emergency or a martial law operate in the whole territory of the Russian Federation, as well as during six months before the term of office of the President expires.

CHAPTER 6. THE GOVERNMENT OF THE RUSSIAN FEDERATION

Article 110

1. The executive power in Russia shall be exercised by the Government of the Russian Federation.

2. The Government of the Russian Federation consists of the Chairman of the Government of the Russian Federation, Deputy Chairman of the Government of the Russian Federation and federal ministries.

Article 111

1. The Chairman of the Government of the Russian Federation shall be appointed by the President of the Russian Federation with the consent of the State Duma.

2. The proposal on the candidate to the post of the Chairman of the Government of the Russian Federation shall be submitted not later than two weeks after a newly-elected President of the Russian Federation takes office or after the resignation of the Government of the Russian Federation or one week after the State Duma rejects the candidate.

3. The State Duma shall consider the candidate nominated by the President of the Russian Federation for the post of the Chairman of the Government of the

Russian Federation during week after the submission of the nomination.

4. In case the State Duma rejects three times the candidates for the post of the Chairman of the Government of the Russian Federation, dissolve the State Duma and appoint new elections.

Article 112

1. Not later than a week after appointment shall submit to the President of the Russian Federation proposals on the structure of the federal bodies of executive power.

2. The Chairman of the Government of the Russian Federation shall propose to the President of the Russian Federation candidates for the posts of Deputy chairmen of the Government of the Russian Federation and federal ministries.

Article 113

According to the Constitution of the Russian Federation, the federal laws and decrees of the President of the Russian Federation the Chairman of the Government of the Russian Federation shall determine the guidelines of the activities of the Government of the Russian Federation and organize its work.

Article 114

1. The Government of the Russian Federation shall:

a) work out and submit to the State Duma the federal budget and ensure its implementation, submit to the State Duma a report on the implementation of the federal budget;

b) ensure the implementation in the Russian Federation of a single financial, credit and monetary policy;

c) ensure the implementation in the Russian Federation of a single state policy in the sphere of culture, science, education, health protection, social security and ecology;

d) manages the federal property;

e) carry out measures to secure the defence of the country, the state security, and the implementation of the foreign policy of the Russian Federation;

f) implement measures to ensure the rule of law, human rights and freedoms, protection of property and public order, and crime control;

g) exercise other powers vested in it by the Constitution of the Russian Federation, the federal laws and decrees of the President of the Russian Federation.

2. The rules of activities of the Government of the Russian Federation shall be determined by the federal constitutional law.

Article 115

1. On the basis and for the sake of implementation of the Constitution of the Russian Federation, the federal laws, normative decrees of the President of the Russian Federation the Government of the Russian Federation shall issue decisions and orders and ensures their implementation.

2. The decisions and orders of the Government of the Russian Federation shall be obligatory for fulfillment in the Russian Federation.

3. The decisions and orders of the Government of the Russian Federation, if they are inconsistent with the Constitution of the Russian Federation, federal laws and decrees of the President of the Russian Federation, may be cancelled by the President of the Russian Federation.

Article 116

The Government of the Russian Federation shall resign before a newly-elected President of the Russian Federation.

Article 117

1. The Government of the Russian Federation may offer to resign and the President of the Russian Federation either shall accept or reject the resignation.

2. The President of the Russian Federation may take a decision on the resignation of the Government of the Russian Federation.

3. The State Duma may express no-confidence to the Government of the Russian Federation. A no-confidence resolution shall be adopted by a majority of votes of the total number of the deputies of the State Duma. After the State Duma expresses no-confidence to the Government of the Russian Federation, the President of the Russian Federation shall be free to announce the resignation of the Government or to reject the decision of the State Duma. In case the State Duma again expresses no-confidence to the Government of the Russian Federation during three months, the President of the Russian Federation shall announce the resignation of the Government or dissolve the State Duma.

4. The Chairman of the Government of the Russian Federation may raise before the State Duma the issue of no-confidence to the Government of the Russian Federation. If the State Duma votes no-confidence, the President shall adopt in seven days a decision on the resignation of the Government of the Russian Federation or dissolve the State Duma and announce new elections.

5. In case of a resignation of the Government of the Russian Federation it shall continue to work on the instruction of the President of the Russian Federation until a new Government of the Russian Federation is formed.

CHAPTER 7. JUDICIAL POWER

Article 118

1. Justice in the Russian Federation shall be administered by courts alone.

2. The judicial power shall be exercised by means of constitutional, civil, administrative and criminal proceedings.

3. The judicial system of the Russian Federation shall be instituted by the Constitution of the Russian Federation and the federal constitutional law. The creation of extraordinary courts shall not be allowed.

Article 119

Judges may be citizens of the Russian Federation over 25 years of age with a higher education in law and a law service record of not less than five years. The federal law may introduce additional requirements for judges of the courts of the Russian Federation.

Article 120

1. Judges shall be independent and submit only to the Constitution and the federal law.

2. If after considering a case, the court of law decides that an act of a state or other body contradicts the law, it shall pass an appropriate decision according to the law.

Article 121

1. Judges shall be irremovable.

2. The powers of a judge be ceased or suspended only on the grounds and according to the rules fixed by the federal law.

Article 122

1. Judges shall possess immunity.

2. A judge may not face criminal responsibility otherwise than according to the rules fixed by the federal law.

Article 123

1. Examination of cases in all courts shall be open. Examinations in camera shall be allowed only in cases envisaged by the federal law.

2. Trial by default in criminal courts shall not be allowed except in cases fixed by the federal law.

3. Judicial proceedings shall be held on the basis of controversy and equality of the parties.

4. In cases fixed by the federal law justice shall be administered by a court of jury.

Article 124

The courts shall be financed only from the federal budget and the possibility of the complete and independent administration of justice shall be ensured in keeping with the requirements of federal law.

Article 125

1. The Constitution Court of the Russian Federation consists of 19 judges.

2. The Constitution Court of the Russian Federation upon requests of the President of the Russian Federation, the Council of the Federation, the State Duma, one fifth of the members of the Council of the Federation or of the deputies of the State Duma, the Government of the Russian Federation, the Supreme Court of the Russian Federation and the Higher Arbitration Court of the Russian Federation, the bodies of legislative and executive power of the subjects of the Russian Federation shall consider cases on the correspondence to the Constitution of the Russian Federation of:

a) the federal laws, normative acts of the President of the Russian Federation, the Council of the Federation, the State Duma, the Government of the Russian Federation;

b) the constitutions of republics, charters, and also the laws and other normative acts of the subjects of the Russian Federation adopted on the issues under the jurisdiction of the bodies of state authority of the Russian Federation or under the joint jurisdiction of the bodies of state authority of the Russian Federation and the bodies of state authority of the subjects of the Russian Federation;

c) the treaties concluded between the bodies of state authority of the Russian Federation and the bodies of state authority of the subjects of the Russian Federation, the treaties concluded between the bodies of state authority of the subjects of the Russian Federation;

d) international treaties and agreements of the Russian Federation which have not come into force.

3. The Constitution Court of the Russian Federation shall resolve disputes on jurisdiction matters:

a) between the federal bodies of state authority;

b) between the bodies of state authority of the Russian Federation and the bodies of state authority of the subjects of the Russian Federation;

c) between the higher bodies of state authority of the subjects of the Russian Federation.

4. The Constitution Court of the Russian Federation, upon complaints about violations of constitutional rights and freedoms of citizens and upon court requests shall check, according to the rules

fixed by the federal law, the constitutional of a law applied or subject to be applied in a concrete case.

5. The Constitution Court of the Russian Federation, upon the requests of the President of the Russian Federation, the Council of the Federation, the State Duma, the Government of the Russian Federation, the bodies of the legislative power of the subjects of the Russian Federation, shall give its interpretation of the Constitution of the Russian Federation.

6. Acts or their certain provisions recognized as unconstitutional shall become invalid; international treaties and agreements not corresponding to the Constitution of the Russian Federation shall not be liable for enforcement and application.

7. The Constitution Court of the Russian Federation, upon the request of the Council of the Federation, shall provide a conclusion on the observance of the fixed procedure for advancing charges of treason or of another grave crime against the President of the Russian Federation.

Article 126

The Supreme Court of the Russian Federation shall be the supreme judicial body for civil, criminal, administrative and other cases under the jurisdiction of common courts, shall carry out judicial supervision over their activities according to federal law-envisaged procedural forms and provide explanations on the issues of court proceedings.

Article 127

The Higher Arbitration Court of the Russian Federation shall be the supreme judicial body for settling economic disputes and other cases examined by courts of arbitration, shall carry out judicial supervision over their activities according to federal law-envisaged procedural forms and provide explanations on the issues of court proceedings.

Article 128

1. The judges of the Constitution Court of the Russian Federation, the Supreme Court of the Russian Federation, the Higher Arbitration Court of the Russian Federation shall be appointed by the Council of the Federation upon the proposals by the President of the Russian Federation.

2. Judges of other federal courts shall be appointed by the President of the Russian Federation according to the rules fixed by the federal law.

3. The powers, the rules for forming and functioning of the Constitution Court of the Russian Federation, of the Supreme Court of the Russian Federation and the Higher Arbitration Court of the Russian Federation shall be fixed by the federal constitutional law.

Article 129

1. The Procurator's Office of the Russian Federation shall form single centralized structure in which procurators are subordinate to superior procurators and the Procurator-General of the Russian Federation.

2. The Procurator-General of the Russian Federation shall be appointed and dismissed by the Council of the Federation upon the proposal of the President of the Russian Federation.

3. The procurators of the subjects of the Russian Federation shall be appointed by the Procurator-General of the Russian Federation by agreement with the subjects.

4. Other procurators shall be appointed by the Procurator-General of the Russian Federation.

5. The powers, organization and the rules of the functioning of the Procurator's Office of the Russian Federation shall be determined by the federal law.

CHAPTER 8. LOCAL SELF-GOVERNMENT

Article 130

1. Local self-government in the Russian Federation shall ensure the independent solution by the population of the issues of local importance, of possession, use and disposal of municipal property.

2. Local self-government shall be exercised by citizens through a referendum, election, other forms of direct expression of the will of the people, through elected and other bodies of local self-government.

Article 131

1. Local self-government shall be administered in urban and rural settlements and in other areas with the consideration of the historical and other local traditions. The structure of local self-government bodies shall be determined by the population independently.

2. Changes in borders of the areas in which local self-government is administered shall be made with the consideration of the opinion of the population of the corresponding areas.

Article 132

1. The local self-government bodies shall independently manage municipal property, form, adopt and implement the local budgets, introduce local taxes and dues, ensure the protection of public order, and also solve other issues of local importance.

2. The local self-government bodies may be vested by law with certain state powers and receive the necessary material and financial resources for their implementation. The implementation of the delegated powers shall be controlled by the State.

Article 133

Local self-government in the Russian Federation shall be guaranteed by the right for judicial protection, for a compensation for additional expenses emerging as a result of decisions adopted by state authority bodies, by a ban on the limitations on the rights of local self-government fixed by the Constitution of the Russian Federation and the federal laws.

CHAPTER 9. CONSTITUTIONAL AMENDMENTS AND REVIEW OF THE CONSTITUTION

Article 134

Proposals on amendments and review of the provisions of the Constitution of the Russian Federation may be submitted by the President of the Russian Federation, the Council of the Federation, the State Duma, the Government of the Russian Federation, the legislative (representative) bodies of the subjects of the Russian Federation, and also by groups numbering not less than one fifth of the number of the members of the Council of the Federation or of the deputies of the State Duma.

Article 135

1. Provisions of Chapters 1, 2 and 9 of the Constitution of the Russian Federation may not be revised by the Federal Assembly.

2. If a proposal on the review of the provisions of Chapters 1, 2 and 9 of the Constitution of the Russian Federation is supported by three fifths of the total number of the members of the Council of the Federation and the deputies of the State Duma, then according to federal constitutional law a Constitutional Assembly shall be convened.

3. The Constitutional Assembly shall either confirm the invariability of the Constitution of the Russian Federation or draft a new Constitution of the Russian Federation, which shall be adopted by the Constitutional Assembly by two thirds of the total number of its members or submitted to a referendum. In case of a referendum the Constitution of the Russian Federation shall be considered adopted, if over half of the voters who came to the polls

supported it and under the condition that over half of the electorate participated in the referendum.

Article 136

Amendments to the provisions of Chapters 3-8 of the Constitution of the Russian Federation shall be adopted according to the rules fixed for adoption of federal constitutional laws and come into force after they are approved by the bodies of legislative power of not less than two thirds of the subjects of the Russian Federation.

Article 137

1. Amendments in Article 65 of the Constitution of the Russian Federation determining the structure of the Russian Federation shall be introduced on the basis of the federal constitutional law on the admission to the Russian Federation and the creation of new subjects of the Russian Federation within it, on changes in the constitutional-legal status of a subject of the Russian Federation.

144

2. In case changes are made in the name of a Republic, territory, region, city of federal importance, autonomous region or autonomous area, the new name of the subject of the Russian Federation shall be included in Article 65 of the Constitution of the Russian Federation.

SECOND SECTION

CONCLUDING AND TRANSITIONAL PROVISIONS

1. The Constitution of the Russian Federation shall come into force from the moment of its official publication according to the results of a nationwide referendum.

The day of the nationwide referendum of December 12, 1993 shall be considered to be the day of adopting the Constitution of the Russian Federation.

Simultaneously the Constitution (Fundamental Law) of the Russian Federation - Russia, adopted on April 12, 1978 with all amendments and changes, shall become invalid.

In case of non-compliance with the Constitution of the Russian Federation of the provisions of the

Federal treaty - the Treaty on the Division of Subjects of Jurisdiction and Powers Between the Federal Bodies of State Power of the Russian Federation and the Bodies of Authority of the Sovereign Republics within the Russian Federation, the Treaty on the Division of Subjects of Jurisdiction and Powers Between the Federal Bodies of State Power of the Russian Federation and the Bodies of Authority of the Territories, Regions, Cities of Moscow and St. Petersburg of the Russian Federation, the Treaty on the Division of Subjects of Jurisdiction and Powers Between the Federal Bodies of State Power of the Russian Federation and the Bodies of Authority of the Autonomous Region, and Autonomous Areas within the Russian Federation, and also other treaties concluded between the federal bodies of state authority of the Russian Federation and bodies of state authority of the subjects of the Russian Federation, treaties between the bodies of state authority of the subjects of the Russian Federation, the provisions of the Constitution of the Russian Federation shall be applicable.

2. The laws and other legal acts acting in the territory of the Russian Federation before the given Constitution comes into force shall be applied in that part which does not contradict the Constitution of the Russian Federation.

3. The President of the Russian Federation, elected according to the Constitution (Fundamental Law) of the Russian Federation - Russia, since the given Constitution comes into force, since carry out the powers fixed in it until the term of office for which he was elected expires.

4. The Council of Ministers (Government) of the Russian Federation from the moment when the given Constitution comes into force shall acquire the rights, obligations and responsibilities of the Government of the Russian Federation fixed by the Constitution of the Russian Federation and since then shall be called the Government of the Russian Federation.

5. The courts of the Russian Federation shall administer justice according to their powers fixed by the given Constitution.

After the Constitution comes into force, the judges of all the courts of the Russian Federation shall retain their powers until the term they were elected for expires. Vacant positions shall be filled in according to the rules fixed by the given Constitution.

6. Until the adoption and coming into force of the federal law establishing the rules for considering cases by a court of jury, the existing rules of court examination of corresponding cases shall be preserved.

Until the criminal procedure legislation of the Russian Federation is brought into conformity with the provisions of the present Constitution, the previous rules for arrest, detention and keeping in custody of people suspected of committing crime shall be preserved.

7. The Council of the Federation of the first convocation and the State Duma of the first convocation shall be elected for a period of two years.

8. The Council of the Federation shall meet in its first sitting on the thirtieth day after its election. The first sitting of the Council of the Federation shall be opened by the President of the Russian Federation.

9. A deputy of the State Duma of the first convocation may be simultaneously a member of the Government of the Russian Federation. The provisions of the present Constitution on the immunity of deputies in that part which concerns the actions (inaction) connected with fulfillment of office duties shall not extend to the deputies of the State Duma, members of the Government of the Russian Federation.

The deputies of the Council of the Federation of the first convocation shall exercise their powers on a non-permanent basis.